HOW TO IMPROVE YOUR SCHOOL
How can you raise standards in your school?

This book takes a practical look at how improvements can be made in any school.

It cuts through the jargon of the specialist and shows how ideas and intentions can be turned into direct actions that will help a school improve its performance and effectiveness.

As well as addressing headteachers and governors, the book will also provide invaluable guidance for all those who work in and with schools.

Current issues of debate are dealt with in a clear and informative way. There are chapters on:

- effective schools and how they have acheived their goals
- leadership within schools
- making critical interventions to secure improvement
- teaching and learning effectively
- how schools involve others to aid improvement

This is a book that no school will want to be without. It is essential reading for everyone involved in education.

Tim Brighouse is Chief Education Officer for Birmingham City Council, and joint vice-chair of the government's Standards Task Force. **David Woods** is a Senior Education Adviser at the DfEE and was previously head of the Birmingham Advisory and Support Service.

Education

This book is dedicated to all those who work, teach and learn in Birmingham's schools and contribute so much energy, effort and love to the transformation of children's and young people's achievement.

HOW TO IMPROVE YOUR SCHOOL

Tim Brighouse and David Woods

London and New York

First published 1999
by Routledge
11 New Fetter Lane, London EC4P 4EE

Simultaneously published in the USA and Canada
by Routledge
29 West 35th Street, New York, NY 10001

Reprinted 1999

Routledge is an imprint of the Taylor & Francis Group

© 1999 Tim Brighouse and David Woods

Typeset in Garamond by
M Rules
Printed and bound in Great Britain by MPG Books, Bodmin, Cornwall

British Library Cataloguing in Publication Data
A catalogue record for this book is available from the British Library

Library of Congress Cataloging in Publication Data
Brighouse, Tim
How to improve your school/Tim Brighouse and David Woods.
p. cm.
Includes bibliographical references (p.) and index.
ISBN 0–415–19444–X (alk. paper)
1. School improvement programs – Great Britain.
2. Educational leadership – Great Britain.
I. Woods, David, 1942– . II. Title.
LB2822.84.G7B75 1999
371.2'00941 – dc21
98–34525 CIP

ISBN 0–415–19444–X

CONTENTS

FIGURES AND TABLES

Figures

Tables

ACKNOWLEDGEMENTS

How to Improve your School has been inspired by the ideas and practices of many heads, teachers and advisers working in the City of Birmingham and across the whole country.

We would particularly like to thank the City Council and Education Committee of Birmingham for their determined and unswerving support in backing education reform and establishing effective partnerships with schools and all other stakeholders.

Many thanks are also due to Frances Wakefield, Julie Reynolds and Carol Pye, who prepared the manuscript, having first interpreted the writing!

The extract from 'The Cure at Troy' by Seamus Heaney is reprinted by kind permission of Faber & Faber Ltd. Jenny Radley's poem is reprinted by kind permission of the *Times Educational Supplement* (©Times Supplements Limited, 1997).

History says, Don't hope
on this side of the grave
But then, once in a lifetime
The longed for tidal wave
Of justice can rise up,
And hope and history rhyme
Seamus Heaney, *The Cure at Troy*

INTRODUCTION

We have written this book because many people in the last four or five years have asked us to put down on paper some of the things we have often spoken about in Birmingham and around the country at meetings, courses, conferences and whole-school INSET days. Between us we have also written a few articles which can now usefully be brought together.

The book is born from a belief that we are on the edge of a great leap forward in whole-school and pupil success. There are various, complex reasons for that. Information and communications technology must be the equivalent to the invention of the printing press as far as transforming what is possible in teaching and learning. There is a conjunction of time (the millennium) and economic circumstance (the information and technology age has succeeded the service, industrial and agricultural revolutions) which conspires to make education a political imperative in most societies. It has certainly done so in ours, with education at the heart of the government's priorities.

After some 20 years of research and practice, which has produced an impressive range of critical literature, we now also know much more about school effectiveness and school improvement. However, we need to make sure that the knowledge we have is taken up by schools and teachers and all those who work with them.

This book is written particularly for individual schools. We hope that the map we describe will give them the necessary compass points to enable them to check their progress and make useful comparisons with other travellers. This is vital if we are to travel as pilgrims rather than as nomads. We also offer a grammar of school improvement, to provide a common language of analysis, discussion and debate as we go through the various chapters in the book dealing with the parallel worlds of school improvement and school effectiveness, leadership, teaching and learning, interventions, and a consideration of the roles of the various stakeholders. This grammar is made up of the following parts:

- punctuation
  'butterflies', very small initiatives taken by schools which have a disproportionate effect as catalysts for improvement and taken together affect climate

1

- nouns
  the key factors of school effectiveness such as:
  a shared vision and goals
  a positive ethos
  structured sessions for teaching
  high teacher expectations
  pupil's involvement in their learning
  purposeful teaching and learning

- verbs
  the processes of school improvement, described by us as:
  the exercise of leadership
  the practice of management and organisation
  the creation of an environment most suitable for learning
  the practice of collective review
  the practice of teaching and the practice of learning
  staff development
  the development of parental and community involvement

- adjectives
  the descriptors of successful practices, which we illustrate throughout the
  book

- adverbial clauses
  critical interventions which are directly focused changes of policy and
  practice, such as:
  seeking improved standards of attainment through target setting and
  benchmarking
  increasing the range of one-to-one learning opportunities
  whole-school participation in innovation and research
  raising pupil self-esteem

- tenses
  planned changes over time which make up the melodies and rhythms of
  school improvement

It is important to stress that the context of this emphasis on school improvement has been specific in a number of ways, although it has universal application.

Inevitably, our evidence is drawn heavily but not exclusively from Birmingham schools. Birmingham will be seen as, and is, a city of great deprivation. It ranks fifth poorest on the Department of the Environment, Trade and the Regions (DETR) index of social deprivation: it contains the poorest wards in the country. It has a dilapidated housing stock with a massive backlog of repair and rebuilding to be tackled and there are high levels of unemploy-ment in many wards of the city. But it also contains pockets of great affluence, for example in Harborne and Sutton Coldfield, and like all cities it boasts some regional and national examples of common wealth, whether in the concert hall which is home to the City of Birmingham Symphony Orchestra with whom Sir Simon Rattle has made his reputation or in ballet, theatre and sport. The reality, whether in outer ring estates, inner-city Birmingham or the more affluent Sutton Coldfield suburbs, is that Birmingham supplies an example both of the challenge of urban education and of the rather smoother waters found elsewhere. It is from this range of contexts that our conclusions are drawn.

We are convinced, moreover, from evidence from other parts of the country where similar – in some cases identical – approaches are taking place that the issues that we have written about here do help schools to succeed. So the book is written in that context, particularly for headteachers, deputies, teachers, advisers, active governors and interested parents. We hope that they will find it a useful stimulus in their efforts to improve their schools.

Questions and answers

Q.   What is the connection between Birmingham Symphony Hall and the Cizez exhibition of children's art in Vienna in 1932?

A.   The old Howard Street Primary School in Birmingham. Well, it is a long and apparently tall story, but it is a good one because it really is true. It was in Vienna that visiting HMI John Blackie saw children's art so breathtaking that he came back determined to encourage primary schools not to focus exclusively on the three Rs, but to use children's naive natural talent in art to foster their self-esteem and powers of self-expression, to give them the thrill of confidence which comes from harnessing natural artistic ability. He encouraged Peter Stone, then head of Steward Street School, to develop the arts when Alec Clegg was a wartime administrator in Margaret Street. Clegg poached Stone when he went to the West Riding and so influenced and publicised the development of all forms of the arts in primary schools.

You can see the never-ending thread of artistic excellence in Birmingham primary schools today. There is an amazing teacher at one North Birmingham junior school who has written and produced original works for her school involving casts of hundreds, and a teacher in another school who annually reworks Shakespeare with children's help to produce vivid original works of art. They are but two of dozens who are strong on drama. Indeed, it was a teacher in Hall Green Junior School who last year revived with such great success the drama festival in which primary schools delighted each other with their performances. And what is one to make of the youngsters with severe disabilities at Wilson Stuart School who created sound and movement that transformed themselves, and transformed a recent evening at the Albert Hall into a spectacle of breathtaking beauty and celebration? On the same evening there was the chance to bathe in the efforts of some outstanding musicians, all of whom have benefited from our peripatetic music service, which has thrived after delegation and has enormous potential – yet it has scarcely begun to ensure that children from different cultural backgrounds are given every chance to discover their musical talents.

I have vivid memories of a kaleidoscope of learning in the arts. I will shake the kaleidoscope three times. The first memory is of a class of

8-year-olds whose imagination was harnessed by a talented teacher, first to create their own play and then to perform it before an amazed audience of parents and colleagues. The play was the work of the children, although you could see the hand of the teacher. Like all good teachers of the arts, however, she had ensured that the influence was sensitively judged and that it in no way detracted from the raw emotion and stark message of the play, which was about the environment and how the children had carried out on their own accord an audit of how 'future friendly' their school really was.

The second shake of the kaleidoscope is far away from Birmingham and long ago. It was in Didcot in the mid-1980s. I was following a child – pupil pursuits we used to call them – to see how teenagers really felt. This particular teenager was turned off, bored, on the verge of disruption all day and, as I discovered as I got to know him, on the same knife edge in other parts of his life. That is, until suddenly his posture changed, his eyes lit up and we entered 'a cave of feelings' – his words not mine – which was the school's drama studio. It was not so much the studio as the teacher who inspired him. The boy was suddenly, quite simply, a different person, capable of movement and expression, of teamwork and of creativity that would have astounded all the other teachers he encountered that day and, I expect, his family. In other pupil pursuits similar transforming effects could be seen in the art room. There, through a variety of media, young people who were otherwise switched off found a key to their own self-belief and their particular identity of hope and talent.

My third and final shake of the kaleidoscope is a more recent one, in the Shakespeare Room of the Central Library where Benjamin Zephaniah was reading poetry to a group of young poets from Ladywood School.

Like so many enthusiasts for the arts, especially after the long debate about the first and second National Curriculum, I am glad there is still the courage to back judgement about the importance of the arts as a key to learning for so many young people. That is why we feature the arts within the Primary Guarantee. That is why the city of Birmingham is pleased to co-operate with the West Midlands Arts Council to provide opportunities for joint ventures, especially for artists in residence. That is why the city wants to find ways of supporting initiatives such as theatre-in-education groups, especially, of course, those associated with equal opportunities such as Voice-Box, Language Alive and Big Brum. Some schools use their budget balances really creatively, to transform the learning environment through the arts with bought-in work-shops for three, four or five days, to highlight dance, music, drama, storytelling or artistic creation through various media. The outcome is usually the discovery of young talent which otherwise might be denied us all. Sir Hugh Casson spoke recently of the young autistic genius, Stephen Wiltshire, whose architectural drawings have created almost a new art form. Casson's words were chosen so well as a compliment to the young genius's artistic talent: 'Every now and then' he wrote, 'a rocket of young talent appears and explodes and continues to shower us with its sparks. Stephen Wiltshire is one of those rockets.' Whether in the Ladywood Poetry Festival, in the Broadway Arts Festival with its impressive emphasis on South Asian art or in the many other events happening in our schools, there is no better city or more energetic set of teachers to discover that talent.

1

EFFECTIVE AND IMPROVING SCHOOLS

Parallel fields of research and how they overlap

> The enigma of successful and unsuccessful schools is that we can easily
> recognise them but we forget how their faces acquired the lines of hope-
> ful optimism or pessimistic despair and how they became healthy or ill.

Everyone agrees that successful schools are desirable.

This chapter seeks to establish a language with which we can identify the characteristics of success and a map to guide us through the processes that we necessarily engage in when creating or destroying those characteristics. The rest of the book attempts first to examine two of those processes – the exercise of leadership and the practice of teaching and learning – in some practical depth and then to offer a set, or menu, of small and larger interventions which we have seen offer disproportionate advantage in schools making progress, before finally considering the contribution of stakeholders and partners to school improvement.

Until relatively recently that would not have been possible. Those running the system, headteachers, teachers and governors knew nothing of research into school effectiveness and school improvement. School was a place where something went on beyond the public or private gaze. Children were left at the school gate and stories of what went on inside grew or diminished with the telling, but, in this country at least, nobody much knew or cared what happened behind the classroom door. Strangely, until Michael Rutter published his *Fifteen Thousand Hours* in 1979, the conventional wisdom amongst social scientists was that schools didn't make a significant difference to life's chances. However, after Rutter's work, first as a trickle, then with a rush, the tide of greater understanding of school success has meant that we have gained greater and ever more precise insights into the characteristics of that success and the means of achieving those characteristics.

For many years it used to be the case that for the busy headteacher and staff and for the school governor, the truism much bruited abroad on the Clapham omnibus was a correct one – namely that good schooling 'is all down to the headteacher'. Even now, you will find widespread agreement that that is the top and bottom of it. But it is a bit more complicated than that.

Most people know when they are in a successful school, although it is only obvious after seeing or experiencing a school that is unsuccessful or complacent. The contrast then is stark.

A case of an unsuccessful school

The door bangs. Nobody thinks to hold doors open for the adults. There is litter and noise everywhere: the lavatories are locked; pupils are not allowed into the school at breaktime whatever the weather. Grim-faced adults pass each other in the corridor without a word and try to ignore what is going on, waiting for someone else to sort out the skirmishes that break out among pupils. They seek refuge in the staffroom and share stories, almost like warriors returning from the front. They talk *about* children not *with* them.

Everyone has become accustomed to being late for lessons and the attendance rate of staff nears that of the pupils. You know where the head's study is: there is a long line of miscreants waiting for what the staff believe to be inadequate discipline and attention.

Energy has seeped away from the school. School for most children and staff is a collusive activity. Children are mainly engaged in aimless tasks to occupy their time in the name of consolidating their learning. Staff meetings are concerned with sharing information and the time of managers is taken up with behaviour referrals and awkward parents. All are tired.

OFSTED inspection reports offer less journalistic ways of describing either the unsuccessful school outlined above or the following contrasting successful one described below.

The successful school

Conversations multiply on the way into school. All children make their way, each in their own style, some busy and smart, others inarticulate and dishevelled, to their tutor group where the teacher silently ticks off their arrival while engaging in encouragingly casual conversation: 'Shane – good to see you back! Your cold's better? See you at practice tonight – got your boots?' It is the same in all classrooms: the registration is the accumulation of special personal and social information locked into

---

the database of the teacher, to be used to good effect in teaching and learning. Some reluctant 'anoraks' are shooed from the open learning centre by the senior teacher. Corridors are places where unconsidered trifles create the vital social cement and minute adjustments are quickly agreed to the school's tactics for each child. There is a silent expectation at school assemblies – the chance acknowledged by the majority of participants for both a vivid shared tale which may involve adults, pupils or a mixture of the two together with music and a celebration of collective and individual achievements. The school visually gives a statement of its priorities, whether in the outstanding artwork or in the displays of pupil and adult achievement or in the news about school clubs or societies, or of language and maths policies, and most tellingly, of the shared behaviour code framed in the first person plural to incorporate adults and pupils alike. It is a place of optimism and pace; laughter abounds and can be relied upon to overcome the daily crises and the occasional tragedies.

Teachers recall good schools as places which punctuated the high points of their careers, where ideas and new experiences overcame exhaustion. Characters are vivid. Parents know them too, not just because their child has gained by meeting a teacher whose actions have gone far beyond what they had to do but also as places where the school collectively does far more than the minimum. So homework is set and marked; residential visits are organised and take place; celebratory occasions are the opportunity for a majority staff turnout and the car parks are always full of staff cars, early and late. Parents and communities soon notice.

Teachers recall them, parents recognise them: good schools are places where individuals grow by walking the extra mile.

There are, of course, many in-between schools.

School effectiveness: the nouns and adjectives of successful schooling

In the last 20 years, as though for the first time, someone has gradually begun to restore a painting by a hitherto unrecognised master. School effectiveness research has revealed the characteristics – the nouns and adjectives – of successful schooling, illuminating its various stages.

What does Tizard tell us about successful infant and nursery schools?

- pre-school attainments (especially knowledge of letter-sounds and the ability to use words)
- mothers' levels of education
- teachers' expectations (found to be consistently too low)
- parent–teacher co-operation

Peter Mortimore and others tantalise with the characteristics of successful junior schools:

- purposeful leadership by head
- involvement of deputy head
- involvement of teachers
- consistency among teachers
- structured sessions
- intellectually challenging
- work-centred environment
- limited focus in sessions
- maximum communication between teachers and pupils
- parental involvement
- record keeping
- positive climate

At secondary level too there has been guidance from David Smith and Sally Tomlinson on the characteristics of successful inner-city secondary schools:

- leadership and management in the school by:
  the headteacher
  the heads of departments (at secondary level we may have to talk about 'effective departments' rather than effective schools)
- teacher involvement in decision making (in curriculum, methods, organisation, use of resources, whole-school policies)
- climate of respect (teachers–teachers, pupil–pupils, pupils–teachers, teachers–parents, etc), including respect for other cultures, languages, religions, etc.
- positive feedback to and treatment of pupils

All this and much more sprang from the Rutter list of characteristics, which simply affirmed from a study of 12 inner-city London schools that ethos, leadership, staff attitudes and pupil involvement all made a difference.

By the late 1980s, however, people were becoming increasingly uncomfortable with the nouns and adjectives of schools' success. Busy headteachers caught glimpses of the picture, even magnified details. But what they increasingly sought was a set of processes or a compass by which to navigate.

School improvement: the verbs of successful schooling

Increasingly, a school of researchers who had contributed to the nouns and adjectives was seeking to describe the processes – and in particular how to approach those processes – which schools necessarily engage in on a daily basis. The hope was that if we could learn more about how to tackle those processes in the most propitious way, it might be possible to supply some of the would-be successful schools' needs and point the ways in which characteristics of success, on the one hand, could be achieved, and of failure, on the other hand, might be avoided. So, for example, it doesn't take much imagination to spot that characteristics such as the 'involvement of the deputy head', or the 'involvement of the staff' relate to leadership being shared. So *how* leadership is exercised could be a complementary factor so far as the achievement of the characteristics is concerned.

In Birmingham we took the view that there were seven processes which encompassed most activities of school life:

- the practice of teaching and learning
- the exercise of leadership
- the practice of management and organisation
- the practice of collective review
- the creation of an environment most suitable for learning
- the promotion of staff development
- the encouragement of parental and community involvement

There is no sense in which we believe these processes to be the only configuration possible. Others may have better ones. Indeed, there is a need for standard English to replace our Birmingham dialect as soon as possible so that all schools in the United Kingdom have the chance to learn one from another in the 'benchmarking' processes we describe later in chapter 4.

Our purpose in describing these processes is to construct a map, so that schools might have a better chance of understanding:

- how to achieve the characteristics
- the practice of schools in similar or dissimilar circumstances that they might compare notes with – benchmarking
- the findings of researchers

We feel very strongly about the need for this and believe the precedent of the National Curriculum and its assessment arrangements proves the point. There is little doubt in our minds that one of the benefits of the introduction of the National Curriculum and the national framework of assessment has been the way that teachers have found themselves able to compare more precisely with each other what they have taught in terms of skill, competence and

11

understanding, and even more significantly what they understand in terms of pupil progress. Of course the early benefits of the latter were evident to teachers who were fortunate enough to engage in Certificate of Secondary Education (CSE) moderation, and all secondary teachers engaged with this age group were similarly influenced for the better by the introduction of the General Certificate of Secondary Education (GCSE). But after 1989 the same benefits have been extended through Key Stage 1 to early years work. Small wonder, of course, that Key Stage 2 and Key Stage 3 remain points where there is most concern about quality in annual Office for Standards in Education (OFSTED) inspection reports, since they were the last to be affected by the introduction of the National Curriculum and its assessment arrangements and the benefits from mutual moderation and discussion.

So the establishment of a map by which whole-schools may learn from each other is the key both to spreading good practice and to avoiding the self-defeating cycle of painfully and painstakingly learning lessons, only for them to be forgotten, forcing the next generation to learn the same things all over again.

Of the seven processes listed in p. 11, leadership and teaching and learning, are focused on later in this book, so we content ourselves here with the briefest sketches of the other five processes.

The practice of management

Good management may be summarised in the cycle set out in Figure 1.1

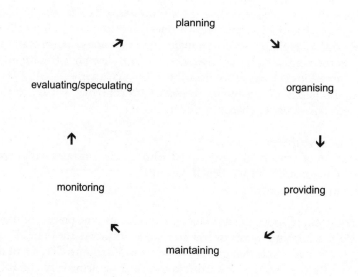

Figure 1.1 The cycle of good management

Clearly, any one of the sub-processes (planning, organising, etc.) in this process is capable of much further elaboration. It will be seen that we have begun to have second thoughts about the cycle's sixth process, evaluating. The problem, so clearly seen in the south-west sector of the quadrant, is an over-emphasis on the judgemental. A manager, whether at departmental, phase or school level, who is given to ideas, certainty and quick decisions might be inclined to undertake the monitoring themselves while the whole affected team remained in ignorance and therefore perhaps unconvinced and alienated by the process. The subsequent evaluation might guide decisions that nobody owned.

We now prefer to substitute the word 'speculate', not because we are opposed to evaluation – indeed, ideally both should be there – but to make a point that management should be as much about questions and promoting a lively debate about the results of the monitoring of evidence as it should be about providing answers.

Management is as much about questions as answers.

Indeed, we can't rid ourselves of the image of the notice on the back of one manager's door:

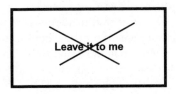

What, of course, the manager is constantly reminding him- or herself of is the danger of relieving others of work and responsibility so that in management terms the school becomes a place which exemplifies the unforgettable words of the visiting school inspector who debriefed a head with the devastating comment: 'Well, the teachers are working very hard, but that is more than can be said for the children.' Moreover, the notice may be a very timely reminder to the head on Friday afternoons not to be the dumping ground for other people's worries as staff seek to unload their intractable problems before a weekend break!

So sharing of management tasks and ownership of the need for them is crucial to a successful school.

When OFSTED reports keep mentioning 'monitoring is in need of development' or even more seriously 'planning', they leave out the salient feature, namely the *collective* nature of the two sub-processes. One of our chosen 'butterflies' later in this book compares and contrasts the judgemental with the speculative – and therefore collective – quality of management.

Without all these sub processes in place, however, the school is adrift in a sea of value judgements and a cacophony of personal prejudice, both in assessing its own processes and in forming an adjustment to the new direction of its actions.

I take my stand on detail

The words of the Victorian provide a timely reminder to those who are non-completers of tasks and low on organisational skills. School practices and processes which are always 'on a wing and a prayer' are also energy sapping. Meticulous planning and organisation, whether of lessons, assemblies, examinations, school performances, external entries, school meals monies, trips or the myriad of other school activities, are essential. Much of a school's work however, both in learning and teaching can be shared with the support staff of the school.

Attention to detail is immediate. A chronically banging door in the corridor can ruin lessons and therefore the proportion of time learners spend in being surprised into understanding or doing things they thought beyond them. The door needs to be fixed. We remain impressed by schools which are eternally attending to improvements in communication in a systematic way. Communication is never fixed: it's always broken because some people don't hear and others don't listen.

The school staff handbook is therefore a necessary document nowadays, but how it is managed can vary. Most staff handbooks are similar. They encompass a simple mission or vision statement for the school, a list of policies, procedures and practices, some of them for information only. The problem is that most people lose them and they can sometimes become a 'blame and shame' opportunity when managers or leaders talk with each other about – not with – other members of staff. 'Why didn't they read the staff handbook? It is set out clearly . . .' Schools can overcome that by chaining a couple of staff handbooks to the staffroom noticeboard, another to the foyer in the general office and another in each faculty area and meeting room. If the handbook is loose-leaf in a ring binder, colour coded for ease of reference and if each policy starts on a separate sheet, a start has been made in getting the detail right. The detail will be completely right if three further steps are taken. Each policy should have within it a mention of members of staff and the chair whose responsibility it is to convene the next review and the date for it. Second, the policy should be followed by a list of the practices that are carried out annually/termly/ weekly/daily, with the initials for those responsible for maintaining this – usually members of the staff community. Finally, informational staff meetings should have the staff handbook as a standing item (once every term?) so that any changes in the personnel, policy and practice involved can be ceremonially carried out by the chair of the meeting and changes made to every copy used as a reference point.

Governors' meetings too are susceptible to the same treatment. The parents' board in the entrance hall enables similar communication strategies to be facilitated.

Communication doesn't stop with staff handbooks – though get that right as a comprehensive, practical, usable manual and most of the rest will follow – after all, if the handbook is a comprehensive statement of policies and practices, it should. Similar attention to detail, however, needs to be given to:

- the arrangements for staff meetings
- the annual 'rites of passage', e.g. awards evenings, INSET days and other staff development activities
- preparation for and, most importantly, follow through after OFSTED

In the next year or two, one more will be added to the list:

- the use of information communication technology (ICT)

As a means of communication management and learning and teaching ICT bids fair to reduce stress by reducing paper and our capacity to lose it.

Allow for size

Sometimes children – or adults for that matter – learning some new technology demonstrate the simple precept of allowing for size. Two illustrations make the point. A youngster is asked to calculate the cost of a shopping basket with six items in it, one costing £1.50, another £2.00, a third £2.25, a fourth 75p, a fifth £1.00 and the sixth £2.00. The child is then asked to find out how much change he would get from a £10.00 note. Those too slavishly addicted to a calculator will spend too long manipulating keys to come up with the answer which mental arithmetic will more easily and quickly confirm as 50p. Or watch the darts player and ask what role the calculator would have in their slick combination of mental agility and hand–eye coordination.

Similar over-dependence on the calculator can be seen in many managerial situations where broad, ballpark estimates are enough; so too with ICT. Sometimes we can become slaves to the need for a software system to carry out a management task which may be urgent and needs quick and easy completion. A second illustration makes the point. An authority one of us was involved with ran a teaching agency which eventually was at risk of making a loss on the secondary side, where there were 30 members of staff. The introduction of computerised recording of their take-up by schools (and therefore the possibility of calculating the accumulating deficit) was seen as the answer. And so it may have been, but a quick thought about the small number of staff involved – 30, after all, is a quantum relatively easily comprehended – would have suggested a monthly return, quickly completed by the teachers, with an incentive, of course, for completion, as the solution. That way an accumulating deficit could have been nipped in the bud.

Keep it simple

The point that we are laboriously making is that there is a tendency for over-elaboration and over complication which is cherished by the ineffective, addictive bureaucratic within any system. It needs to be resisted. Size and scale are everything. What is appropriate for a large school is not suitable for a small school; moreover, within a school a necessarily formalised system suitable for whole-school management may be inappropriate for the sub-management activity, whether in a faculty or a phase team.

The practice of collective review

Most schools, through the process of the school development plan, are now involved in the review of their activity in a way that their predecessors were not. The danger is that half the staff are not involved and therefore do not own or reinforce the outcome.

Many heads of faculty or subject co-ordinators in primary school tear their hair in submerged exasperation when the strategy for teaching, for example (do we subtract, do we borrow or do we use decomposition?) is agreed but not followed. Now, clearly, staff who do not have a whole-school policy on that issue which is translated into agreed practice can, and will, confuse children.

> *Collective review is to do with ensuring that the sum of the parts is exceeded by the collective whole.*

It is to do not simply with shared values and systems but with consistent practice.

Collective review, however, is also an opportunity for a school to increase the common wealth of its intellectual curiosity. For, ideally, out of the processes of collective review or self-evaluation will come an extension of knowledge through the sharing of other people's ideas.

Both of us worked for education authorities that pioneered self-evaluation in the early 1980s. Like everything else that is innovatory, the models deployed by those authorities – Solihull and Oxfordshire – had their limitations. Nevertheless, both were intended to come to grips early with the great concern for accountability and to do it in a way which prompted, at the level of the school, professional and properly self-critical review in order to head off what both authorities could see arising, namely imposed external review and regular inspection, with all the negative, punitive side effects which the two authorities guessed would be associated with such a scheme.

So a starting point for collective review essentially boils down to a few simple questions. If the school is collectively reviewing reading, these might run as follows:

- What is our existing reading practice?
  Clearly, in a language/English policy there will be a reading element, so

discussion by the review group will look at the existing practice, perhaps by group discussion, perhaps by shared consideration of simple written statements. Discussion of differences will naturally occur. The second question to the sequence is important too.

- What different practices have we seen in other schools?
  New colleagues are easily drawn in by seeking views of their previous experience, although the best reviews will be based on a report back of 'visits with intent' to other schools by members of staff. 'Visits with intent' is an important phrase. There is no point in people visiting any-where for professional review without a clear and focused brief. Of course, the consideration of the question might prompt such visits. The third question is now brought in to place.

- What advantages and disadvantages do each of these practices have?
  It is at this point that intellectual curiosity, questions and opinions will flow. People have to justify their preference for competing or comple-mentary practices.

There are, however, important things to be noted in the sequence:

- It avoids the 'closing down' effect of judgemental views in the early stages. 'How *well* are we doing something?' is a question which might produce a defensive reaction in insecure colleagues – although in Birmingham we feel that our adoption of the slogan 'improving on previous best' is a useful antidote to that.

- It leads on naturally to the need to collect evidence.
  Any systematic debate on the relative merits of competing practices is unlikely to end without someone wanting to quantify or assess the impact on the children's learning of either one particular course of action or the priority in time and effort to be given to it.

Now therefore, through collective review, staff are in the interesting final ter-ritory in the following sequence:

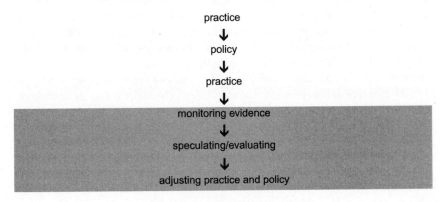

practice
↓
policy
↓
practice
↓
monitoring evidence
↓
speculating/evaluating
↓
adjusting practice and policy

The more *collective* these final processes can be, the better. 'Seeing (after all) is believing.'

The place of the critical friend

In this process, a mature school will usually start to seek the views of outsiders in either the monitoring or the speculating on evaluating of evidence collected. It is important in our view that the school at this point involves a person whom it trusts, who is in effect a 'critical friend'. We are both impressed by Michael Fullan's counterpoint of the 'critical friend' with the 'uncritical lover' or the 'unloving critic'. Both the latter are dangerous to the internal health of the school (See chapter 5, pp. 148–150.)

The critical friend at the point of collective review has the quality that staff recognise in themselves when teaching. The critical friend can judge when to tell you how it is without tramping down self-esteem. Most importantly too, they can usually intervene with the right sort of question at the right time to pitch collective expectation just ahead of collective self-esteem, in order that the school can grow.

Don't attempt to do it all at once

One of the mistakes we made all those years ago in the authorities where schools pioneered school self-evaluation was to believe that you could review everything simultaneously. To keep self-review at a sustainable level requires a calendar (usually nowadays embodied in a school development plan) which sees self review embodied in the warp and weft of school life. Moreover, it will affect individual learning plans as much as the collective life of the school, so that pupils self-review their work as a precursor to external marking just as departments, phase teams and whole schools do so collectively. To do otherwise is to introduce dangerous discontinuity of action plans and principles. Such a precept will affect the work of governors too.

One caveat to the proposition that self-review should be intertwined with the rhythm of the school's life, not tackled all at once, must be aired. The need for public accountability in recent years has introduced a necessary but sometimes jarring and often dislocating competing rhythm through the pub-lication of league tables of test or examination scores and regular OFSTED inspection visits. These represent snapshots on the one hand of a part of school life, and on the other (OFSTED) of the school as a whole. Nevertheless, schools that are self-reviewing should regard these occasions as *summative* review occasions. Moreover, if there is a change in OFSTED to focusing on accrediting school self-review as a precursor to inspection, it will be impor-tant to spell out the distinction between the regular, timetabled pattern of review and the summative snapshots. To confuse the two is to introduce dan-gerous overload.

Off the shelf schemes can get you moving

Most schools find it difficult to establish a virtuous cycle of self-review and then to sustain it. From GRIDS (Guidelines for review and internal development in schools) or Quality Development to many others, such as those promoted by the Royal Mail, TSB/Lloyds or individual local authorities and professional associations, there is no shortage of models, each with different and particular strengths from which any school can choose. Most contain wise advice on the way to start the process in a 'stuck' school.

Creating an environment most suitable for learning

Our next process is perhaps the easiest to accomplish – at least as far as two of its three aspects are concerned. The three aspects are:

- the visual
- the aural
- the behavioural

The visual environment

There is much experience on the importance of the visual environment inside the school. Primary schools have taught us much. For them it probably all started with the Cizec exhibition of children's art in Vienna in the 1930s, an event attended by a cluster of imaginative and influential HMIs led by John Blackie, who was later to be Senior Chief Primary Inspector. He recruited to his ranks the likes of Robin Tanner, a great artist in his own right as well as a teacher, and Christian Scheller. All three were to be profoundly influential.

There emerged a group of primary practitioners who were deeply convinced that artistic expression represented a rich vein of children's talent which could be tapped very early, when inhibition was less intrusive. On the child's confidence through the successful use of various media in artistic form could be built success in the other talents such as reading and writing, which our schooling system naturally emphasises. There is much in the argument, even if the release of artistic achievement at a young age often flatters to deceive so far as the talent is concerned. Nevertheless, what emerged were generations of primary teachers who gave ample rein to artistic expression. Through their training and their practice they learnt the skills and techniques of good display.

It has therefore become the rule rather than the exception that the primary classroom and school itself have become a visual delight, often obscure in its purpose; secondary colleagues and a wider public tend to use the pejorative term 'decoration'. Yet look beyond the camouflage of the primary school and you can see its skills. For example, the entrance foyer will illustrate various themes of the school curriculum or community activity. There will be evidence of practice in various media. In individual classrooms, it is as well to notice whether all the children's work is displayed. Moreover, has it avoided the trap of those early artistic enthusiasts who celebrated only art and literary forms? Is there a mathematics puzzle or two? What of scientific work? And the successful primary school will occasionally turn the whole school display activity for half a term to a linked theme which supports a planned set of explorations or values of the whole school or community.

In the individual primary school classroom the environment is planned to encourage the child to autonomous learning: the child is urged to know where material equipment and other learning resources are kept and to take responsibility not only individually in their use, but collectively in their organisation and conservation. You will come across groups of children debating the work exhibited and visiting parents will proudly be shown their own and their friends' efforts. Sometimes in the best reception and infant classrooms, the whole room will be transformed with huge models into some strange and exhilarating exhibit which reinforces the children's learning from a visit. I remember entering a classroom which was a local coalmine, another a farm and yet another a theme park.

In the best run primary schools, the school as a whole is a reflection of the individual classroom, larger but gaining in the process.

At secondary schools such individual and whole-school environmental policies are the exception rather than the rule. Why is that? First, the primary teacher, through the Cizec–Blackie tradition, has been initiated into the importance of the visual in training, and almost all primary teachers have had longer training, on average, than their secondary colleagues. Most of the latter, with the exception of some in the expressive arts, have experienced hardly more than a passing mention of the techniques of display in their training. Second, of course, subject specialisms with their deep knowledge bias demand so much time and attention that the more general 'whole-school' issues get lost. Moreover, secondary heads had for years come from that tradition, oblivious of their surroundings, as a visit to the headteacher's study would easily confirm. It is, for example, still sadly rare to find the secondary headteacher's study wall deliberately exhibiting, on a rolling basis, examples of children's work, and where it does happen it will so often be just art. We say 'just art' not because that is unimportant but because it shows that the head has not taken on board the much wider message of the question of display.

In a secondary school four years ago, an incoming head transformed a desert of an entrance hall one weekend with a couple of cheerful staff volunteers: the children now gain experience in receiving visitors – a job strategically chosen for the third year. After all, if any one group of children are at risk of losing motivation it is Year 9. They look after all the telephones too: it is all part of a carefully structured curriculum in Year 9, designed to find ways of capitalising on their achievements, and part of an intensive review of their strengths and weaknesses with extra teaching available to get them ready for the two years running up to GCSEs.

The same headteacher, a woman (it is significant that most visually aware heads we know in secondary schools tend to be women) soon tackled the visual environment systematically, an initiative she had first raised – we suspect among other things – in the individual, informal 'get-to-know-you' discussions which are a feature of the first year of all new headteachers.

From these she found she had a team of six members of staff, across all departments except science, who had expressed keen interest in matters connected with environmental display or environmental teaching. Moreover, a cursory check of classrooms bore out their practice. She invited them in for a chat one lunchtime and talked to them first of their individual visions and then, skilfully, of what emerged as their collective vision but was, we suspect, hers all along. She promised to speak to the heads of faculties concerned, who were only too pleased to let their enthusiastic colleagues spread illustrations of their skills to the common areas of the faculties.

Already we have missed a step in the story – the science department. It was agreed that the probationary science teacher should be invited to be involved because there was no obvious person among the other members of staff. She was provided with extra INSET on the issue – as it happens from her partner who was a primary-trained teacher in a nearby school. The science team chose the topic for display and the probationer, along with some student teachers at the school, mounted it.

That is how it all started. Now four years on, the school has children's work expertly displayed during three half terms in the year. They have considered the checklist of questions set out on p. 51. Now all the staff – well, all but six old reprobates who claim they cannot learn new tricks but are being increasingly joked out of it – are involved in an end-of-session review of the work displayed.

The aural environment

The aural environment too is susceptible, though less often in our experience, to being a straightforward process that a school might seek to change.

Carpeting your classrooms and corridors can make a huge difference to the behaviour of adults and pupils alike. The echoing cacophony of scraping chairs and competing voices is best recalled in the image of post-war dining halls during a wet 'dinner time' – still of course with us in some cases! The same feature is equally enervating, but on a quiet rather than acute basis, in the unco-operative classroom alongside a long echoing corridor that acts as a thoroughfare for a substantial number of children on a regular basis and a sounding board for noise. Punctuate that everyday classroom story with a bell every 35 or 50 minutes and you have a recipe for diminishing the number of moments children are surprised into doing or understanding something they thought beyond their ability.

Our technology has now reached the point where a lesson's end can be signalled to a teacher alone rather than to the whole school community, either by a remote electronically operated device with a receiver on the wrist or by a flashing light in the top corner of the room, perhaps with a low pitched musical accompaniment. Just as people scorned carpets 20 years ago but now take them for granted as an aid to teaching, so the technological replacement of the lesson bell will be seen as natural five years from now.

The aural environment does not stop there.

Early years teachers use certain sorts of music to affect pupil behaviour: 'I find the children respond to the music I use in the classroom just as they do in assembly and when we take them to the hall for music and movement sessions. I use it in the classroom to practise listening, fine motor movement and as an aid to storytelling with the whole class,' is how one reception class teacher explained it. Then there was the secondary headteacher who, as so many do now, had employed a consultant to run workshops for youngsters in Years 10 and 11, to help them with the memory development techniques associated with learning new material and revision. 'I make no bones about it. Anything that seems to help I'll try,' she declared when explaining that she now personally gave a tape of baroque music to each Year 11 student every September.

We came across a brief theoretical explanation of this use of music to aid learning. According to Lozanov, a Bulgarian psychologist who had startling success in teaching students a new language, you can use what he calls 'passive' concerts (typically of baroque music) both to consolidate the learning of language (and presumably other new material) and as a background which for many people aids learning. His list of passive concert music is as follows:

- Vivaldi
  Five Concertos for Flute and Chamber Orchestra

- Handel
  Organ Concerto in B flat major, Op. 7. No. 6

- J S Bach
  Prelude in G Major, 'Dogmatic Chorales'

- Corelli
  Twelve Concerti grossi, Op. 6 Nos. 4, 10, 11, 12

- J S Bach
  Fantasia for Organ in G major
  Fantasia in C minor

- Couperin
  Sonatas for Harpsichord, 'Le Parnasse'
  (Apotheosis of Corelli) and 'L'Estrée'

- J F Rameau
  Concert Pieces for Harpsichord, 'Pièces de Clavecin' Nos.1 and 5

More contentiously, he goes on to argue that one way of learning a new language is to create a play, with words set out in both languages in text form. The teacher then acts out the new language to an 'active concert'. The pieces for this concert are as follows:

- Beethoven
  Piano Concerto, No. 5 in E flat major

- Mozart
  Symphony No. 35 in D major, 'Haffner'
  Symphony No. 38 in D major, 'Prague'

- Haydn
  Violin Concerto No. 1 in C major
  Violin Concerto No. 2 in G major

- Haydn
  Symphony No. 101 in C major, 'L'Horloge' Symphony No. 84 in G major

- Mozart
  Violin Concerto No. 5 in A major
  Symphony No. 28 in C major
  Symphony No. 40 in G minor

- Brahms
  Violin Concerto in D major, Op. 77

Students are encouraged to use the earlier 'passive' concertos for consolidating learning and as background to coursework completion.

We are not sure what to make of all this. If there is something in it, the implications for inner cities (where so many children come from homes where there is a strong community language) are significant. We met a group of Year 11 girls at a city-centre exhibition: they came from the school where the headteacher hands out the tape of baroque music, so we asked them an innocent question to see if their impression corroborated their headteacher's confidence. They were overwhelmingly enthusiastic.

So the potential for the aural environment is considerable. It goes way beyond the use of music to change mood, to utilise the lunch hour or to create some sort of spiritual experience in assemblies.

The behavioural environment

There is, also the behavioural environment however. Of course, the three elements overlap. We have just advanced a case for the use of music, not merely to influence behaviour but to aid learning. And we do need to exemplify the connection between the visual and the behavioural: illustrated playground notices setting out school rules are visually pleasing but also reinforce a subtle point about behavioural policies, namely that they can be framed positively and optimistically rather than as abrupt commands given by one set of occupants of the school community to another.

Most people, when it comes to behavioural issues, will focus on the children, but we have noticed that in successful schools there is no discontinuity between the way the pupils are treated and treat each other and the way adults are treated and treat each other. If a school staff respect each other, reinforce each other's achievements, try to bite back criticism in public and are themselves celebrated and valued, as individuals and collectively, they are far more likely to approach pupil discipline in the same way.

So the assemblies, the awards evenings, the monitoring of the balance between positive and negative awards for work, attendance, kindness to others, are all part and parcel of the approach. So too is the development of nurturing groups, especially for young children who come from insecure backgrounds – groups designed to enable them to learn how to handle emotions. In the last 20 years we have become much more skilled at the creation of a climate fit for learning, because we have needed to be so in a less deferential, more disputatious and argumentative age. So 'circle time', 'schools' councils', 'pupils' courts' and 'mediation' all spring to mind as examples of interventions which different schools have deployed in order to ensure that at a whole-school level the environment is behaviourally fit for learning and teaching. Of course, such approaches also reinforce the development of citizenship. 'Assertive discipline' from the United States is perhaps the most interesting recent development, partly because it causes most controversy. The idea of a simple set of offences leading to a predictable set of sanctions has been the elusive eldorado of hard-pressed teachers down the ages. The problem, however, is that no pre-set list is ever free from personal interpretation. Moreover, it conflicts with the annoying but nevertheless real dilemma in which we treat children as they might become rather than as they so infuriatingly sometimes are. From a very early age, children test us to move them from a situation where a negative response is tempting – 'No, don't touch that glass!' – to one where we say, 'Why don't we leave that and look at this?' We know that if we immerse children in negativity they become either defiant, depressed, deviant, or all three.

Moreover, the positive, interrogative response inclines towards self-learning and by its very process involves the questioner – the teacher or the parent – in showing that special optimistic interest in the child which has been the prerequisite for successful learning situations down the ages.

Now all that is romantic. We have all, as parents and teachers, had children who appear to be so damaged by what's going on in their lives (either for the moment or permanently) that there is need for speedy corrective action. Assertive discipline, therefore, has its place but not in metronomic simplicity. Like all behaviour policies, it is a matter of judgement.

Some questions for those who would improve school climate

The visual environment

Who is responsible for display in the school and who else is involved?

Do the pupils themselves have some responsibility in selecting and helping the display in communal areas?

Have we used 'artists in residence', perhaps from the local community or through the Arts Council, to engage youngsters in creating and celebrating something of beauty, for example sculptures, murals, other artworks?

In secondary schools (where it is unlikely that more than a small proportion of staff will have had training in display) how do new members of staff gain training in display as part of their induction?

When did we last use part of an INSET day to debate the visual impact of the school or an inside consultant to lead discussion within departments about display?

Within the classroom, what are the walls used for? Are they used to display all the children's work? Are there some puzzles on the walls? How frequently are displays changed? Is there some unfinished work to debate? In the secondary school does the display reinforce the love of subject? Is it sometimes – say, one half term in two years – part of a deliberately planned whole-school cross-curricular survey? In the primary school, does part of the work reinforce the school's language, maths and science policies as well as perhaps the topic/theme of a group of classes?

Outside the school, who is responsible for the cultivated areas? How do we involve the older generation of the community in the maintenance and development of a part of the school's external environment? If our school is one sea of tarmacadam, how do we break that up? Are there seats for youngsters, especially those not wishing to be swept along in informal team games at break time? Do the midday supervisors know

---

about and contribute to the development of the external environment? What INSET do we arrange for them?

In the professional areas, are the notices cynical or humorous? Are there photocopied articles of interest on the noticeboard?

If our buildings are unremittingly unattractive, what can be done about it [simply]? Can the school be camouflaged by fast growing creepers that don't damage the fabric? What is our strategy for ensuring that we don't become or remain the victims of vandalism?

The aural environment

Are the corridors, even when empty, noisy? If so, what is the strategy for changing that? How much of the school is carpeted? What are the acoustics of the hall and dining area? What simple steps can be taken to make them better – could, for example, the use of display materials help acoustically?

Is there a tannoy system in the school? If so is it needed? Is the internal telephone bell intrusive to lessons? What other matters can be changed to decrease staff stress? What about the tables and chairs? Do doors naturally slam?

Is there a thought-out policy of music for dinner times and for the social areas in breaks before and after school? Is there a mix of pop, jazz, reggae, Eastern and Western classical music? Is some of it youngster-performed and some reproduced? If there has to be a bell to summon youngsters from the field, does it need to be institutional?

The personal environment

Is there a code of conduct which applies to all members of the school community – youngsters, staff, parents, governors?

How do our rites and rituals reflect that code of conduct and the school's statement of principles?

In what ways do we collect evidence with which we can review as objectively as possible the successes and shortfalls in personal standards of behaviour within the school community?

The promotion of staff development

Investors in People is no more than a systematic way of ensuring that people know what the enterprise to which they belong is about as a whole and that they are thereby enabled to take a full part in contributing to its development.

When we talk of school staff or the staffroom we automatically bring to our minds teachers. It is arguable that some of the most vital members of the staff at a school are not teachers at all: many teachers have wryly commented, 'If you really want to find out what is happening in the school it is best to ask the caretaker or the school secretary.' And the comment, which at face value is about communication systems, conceals a more fundamental point. After all, the business of the school – whether it concerns problem children, awkward visitors, the administrative support system, the arrangement for trips, meals, ordering equipment and supplies, dealings with County Hall, diocesan authorities or the DfEE, even governors' meetings – all tends to go through the office. Indeed, if headteachers knew as much about the detail of the school as the secretary/administrator/bursar, they would not be doing their job properly.

And while on the subject of support staff, what of the relatively recently acquired midday supervisors? There is little doubt that their skill, coupled with the impact of the external environment at lunchtimes, has a profound effect on the incidence of bullying in particular and the behaviour of the school in general. So the wise school gives a high priority to the development of midday supervisors' skills and attitudes. Extending their expertise with training to be a part of the learning team of the school pays enormous dividends.

So if the teachers are the people who contribute most to a school's main business – namely unlocking the talent of future generations – it is wise not to forget that the support staff have the potential to contribute significantly to that task. Nor is the contribution exclusively behind the scenes. How children are treated in the school's office, how support staff talk to children in the corridor or on the way to school, how they deal with confidences, all affect children's life chances. What is more, as it is almost always the case that more of such staff than teachers live in the locality, their messages to the local community about what is really happening in the school are crucial. If what follows therefore has teachers mainly in mind, it is because their morale is more vulnerable. At every stage, however, it is necessary to stop and ask whether the same issues affect all members of staff.

Teachers get exhausted where the rest of us merely tire

Teachers know that the inflection of their voice, the movement of an eyebrow and their attitude every minute of every day when they are with the children, affects those children's ability to learn. And they are in contact with children a lot. So teachers get exhausted where the rest of us simply tire. Learning is the whole business of the school: it deserves to be in the forefront of the minds and conversations of all in school who nowadays need to guard against displacing learning by managerial or organisational topics such as 'resource management', 'external relations', and so on.

Unlike teachers, the rest of us, including headteachers, enjoy 'down time' when we are properly involved in activities which do not require us to give of ourselves perpetually: we can work in private.

All staff require four conditions to be satisfied if they are going to carry out their duties effectively. They need:

- responsibility
- permitting circumstances
- new experiences
- respect and recognition

Let us unpick each.

Responsibility

Most people confuse responsibility with work. We quite like the former but are liable to get stressed by too much of the latter. Most of us, with the increased pace of communication, particularly in written form, and with the expansion of knowledge, are not short of work. Indeed, from time to time all of us feel helpless about the things we should have read but haven't. It is particularly difficult for subject specialists, for they have seen their own field of specialism transform itself within a very short space of time – after, a year or two. Publications have proliferated to an extent that it is virtually impossible for a serious scholar to be aware of the contents and impact of all that has been written in his or her subject. This point was brought home vividly on a recent Radio 4 programme about the life of J S B Haldane, when experts agreed that for that very reason, the expansion of specialist knowledge, we should not see again the like of Haldane. It would simply be impossible for one mind, however exceptional it might be, to be at the frontiers of knowledge across a wide field and translate that knowledge in a popular form. So there is far greater stress on teachers than previously when advances in knowledge had not accelerated to the same extent. Add to that the multitude of organisational changes required by legislation – the 1986, 1988, 1992, 1993, 1996, 1997 and 1998 Education Acts, for example – and you have a recipe for acute overload for schools.

Because those in schools tend to be idealists, their inability to cope causes enormous guilt, so it is as well for schools to be clear about the difference between work, of which there is too much, and which causes a feeling of guilt, panic, helplessness and inadequacy, and responsibility, which is often badly distributed. Responsibility for something is, after all, having the final say about it: it is taking the lead and providing a vision of how things could be.

The job description in the 1987 Pay and Conditions Act was so unhelpful to staff development because it didn't, as so many job descriptions do not, draw a distinction between jobs to be done and taking responsibility for them. The wisest schools ensure that the contracts for their teachers emphasise no more than two or three principal accountabilities – matters for which the teacher is the lead person in the school – and three or four secondary accountabilities – matters on which the teacher is a supporting person in the formulation of policy. Those are the important matters: they will give the teacher the energy to contribute to the whole life of the school and in doing so they will also offer the teacher fulfilment and satisfaction.

A sample job description

Apart from taking part in the whole professional life of the school which is committed to successful teaching and learning and requires all members of staff to take on tutorial responsibility and the support of others in the usual administrative matters of the school, you have the following principal accountabilities:

- taking the lead in conjunction with departmental colleagues in establishing the mathematical priorities and practices of the school
- ensuring, in conjunction with departmental colleagues and the school's administration, that the department is adequately staffed and resourced
- as a result of the above, establishing with colleagues and the curriculum leader of the school agreed criteria to show how progressively more children in the school may develop their mathematical talents

You also have the following secondary accountabilities:

- contributing appropriately through the school's curriculum review process to the overall curriculum development of the school
- taking the lead from time to time, with agreed criteria, in planning, organising and reviewing one aspect of cross-curricular work
- taking part in some aspect of extra-curricular activity
- monitoring in support of Miss Julian the effectiveness of the PSE programme in the upper school

---

Of course, the whole issue of responsibility is best tackled at the time people are appointed. The work undertaken in preparing a background 'position statement' for job applicants and the principal and secondary accountability list for the particular post is vital. Moreover, it needs to be shared among all staff. We particularly admired the school which devoted a part of the school noticeboard entirely to that purpose, so that as jobs came up, the fruits of the preparatory work were regularly displayed. Of course, the deputy in charge would draw the attention of the whole staff, as the occasion demanded, to the details for the new vacancy. And in that school the process of appointment meant that those involved in the newcomer's principal and secondary account-abilities would take part in some aspect of the interviewing and appointment process, even when there was only one applicant. (After all, sometimes the wise school knows when not to appoint.)

The school had a system for knowing who was responsible for what and there was an open system of appointments. There were, of course, different ideas about how it could be improved, but they all recognised that it was a better system than they had encountered elsewhere. Significantly, one of the improvements they were considering was the extension of the system to support staff. Let us be clear. They had a similar system, but the jobs were not displayed on the noticeboard. Moreover, cross-membership, involving teaching and support staff in appointment processes is at a very tentative stage, but they argue that it is bound to improve the staff's shared sense of common purpose.

Permitting circumstances

Once teachers (and others) have their responsibilities made clear, they desperately need permitting circumstances. At its simplest this has an obvious meaning. If there are no books, materials or equipment, then the opportunity to teach well is, to say the least, restricted. So the link to the environment is obvious and of primary importance: it is analogous to the basic human need of food and warmth.

Three very important matters sometimes get neglected.

TEAMS

First, there is a need to ensure that teachers can work in teams: that means not merely the obvious clustering of subject-interest rooms so that resources are shared but also how whole year groups will be registered.

- Is there the facility within departments for team teaching if it is needed?
- How can the department or faculty head be given physical help to build teamwork?
- Are there noticeboards which show the intellectual curiosity of the faculty?

- If there is emphasis on the home group or the year group, how are those activities physically fostered?
- Can dining or social areas be used to the advantage of the teaching team effort, either of the department, the year/home group or the school?

THE STAFFROOM

Second, there is the question of the staffroom. Here we shall make enemies. You can gain a pretty strong clue to the school's success by its staffroom. If peer group pressure is an issue among pupils, so it is among staff.

There used to be the bridge corner in our early years of teaching. It was great fun but it was the enemy of real thought and debate. More recently and alarmingly the snooker table and the darts board have emerged. Some people will say we exaggerate. We do not. Quite simply, staffroom conventions, even the walls, are a barometer of a school's success. Conversations can be dominated either by backbiting or by debate about children's progress. There can be social chatter with no cutting edge or debates about interests that might inform the school's progress. Walls can be the repository for the cynical cartoon, or more positively, for the latest 'thought-provoking piece' about some educational matter. Bridge, darts and snooker – and let us be clear, we are devotees of all three – shouldn't dominate. That isn't to say that there shouldn't be some provision for such activities. Why not provide perhaps a separate social area available to staff, parents and pupils alike as part of committed practice? It shouldn't be in a staffroom, however.

THE RESOURCE TECHNICIAN

The third point of neglect in teachers' physical permitting circumstances is their access to a unit staffed by support-staff colleagues who are devoted to the production of materials to support their teaching and children's learning. It is bound up with the question of resource-based learning, or flexible learning, as it is now sometimes called. Teachers will find that the use of such approaches will be considerably enhanced if there is a unit properly organised and devoted to their service. So many of the best intentioned schemes in that direction have foundered on the organisation and provision of support-staff backup. The same problem exists where large schools fail to staff adequately the library or resource centre.

It is important that teachers are encouraged to take risks.

There is, however, something far more important to teachers' permitting circumstances than the physical. Put simply, do teachers work in surroundings in which it is permissible – even encouraged – that they should try out new ideas? After all, in unlocking any child's mind they need to keep fresh their sense of intellectual curiosity: they need to be pushing back the frontiers of their knowledge of how some children learn and how information skills and attitudes can be learnt and developed more successfully. The best teachers take risks – and when they do, they need to know they will be backed.

One headteacher we know put it simply, saying that she really hoped – and told teachers she hoped – that they would take risks but that when it was really risky and might get her into a fix with parents or governors, they would tell her – not that she would stop them, but so that she would be prepared to back them. Amazingly, she would remind them occasionally that she hadn't been taken to the limit of saying 'no' for some time.

New experiences

The third aspect of staff development is the need of all staff for 'new experiences'. People need new experiences to keep them intellectually stimulated. To some extent, of course, that happens in the classroom or in departmental meetings or in whole-school activities. it can be a new job: to make a career in simply one set of school surroundings undoubtedly is less broadening than to have experience of three, four or five different settings. Teachers and others argue long and hard about 'fly-by-nights' or people 'who think only of their career' and they denigrate those who hop from one position to another without ever staying long enough to prove anything. Certainly, a stay of less than three, four or five years in one set of circumstances is unlikely to mean that you give as much as you receive. Get much beyond seven, eight or nine years, however, and there is a real risk of becoming stale.

Mrs Hughes is the head of a primary school. When she arrived she inherited staff all of whom had been at the school in the same classrooms for at least eight years. They sat in the staffroom in the same chairs. All were in their mid-thirties and forties. After she had talked to all of them individually she didn't have to prompt three of the staff who separately asked if they could do something more than teach the same age of children, in the same room, in the same way for the next 20 years! It was natural and easy, by teaching their classes, for the head to get the three to start discussions on the various differences between 6–8 and 10-year-olds respectively, the age-groups which happened to be their responsibility. Soon they suggested a change of teaching for a year. Before long two other members of staff were asking to have the same opportunity. Even the remaining three could be persuaded to change classrooms.

At secondary level such changes are easier to engineer, either at the departmental or school level, simply because the school's timetable will require some change of teaching experience from year to year. In one secondary school some of the responsibilities are swapped every three years so that new eyes can be brought to the development of the same problem. Often this is restricted to the senior management team of three, four or five. It is perfectly possible, however, to design principal or secondary accountabilities which can be shared at all levels of staff management. It is necessary to be quite firm about the need for colleagues to try something new, otherwise there is a real danger that work is something that is done almost on automatic pilot and that the only sources of stimulation and new experiences come from outside school, in their home lives.

Of course you know you are on a winner when you find members of staff who, off their own bat, ask if they can try out something new in the school, either as an extra-curricular club or as a different set of teaching experiences. The teacher we met before the summer holidays, sitting on a wall in a Stoke-on-Trent high school, was a headteacher's dream. She was off to the deserts of America for her summer holidays, she said. It was part pleasure, but part the need she feels to have vivid experiences which will excite her teaching in the forthcoming year. In exactly the same way you will be able to spot the long-suffering spouse of a primary teacher who is always collecting things on holidays.

Above all, however, under the need for new experiences, it is essential to enter a plea for a proper set of experiences under the broad heading of INSET. Teachers, just like any other staff, need to have the stimulation of a fresh slant on old ideas and the chance to learn new skills.

Respect and recognition

The fourth need of staff is for respect and recognition.

Simply because teaching is a fairly isolated activity, its success needs to be recognised. There is precious little respect and recognition for teachers, as the following lovely poem from the *TES* so graphically illustrates.

'Who'd be a teacher?' is what we've all said.
When at something past midnight we've crawled into bed,
And thought of the morrow with certain misgivings:
This can't be the best way to earn me a living.
'Who'd be a teacher?' I'm sure you've exclaimed,
When once more in the papers the teachers are blamed
For hooligans, drugs and graffiti, and crimes;
It must be our fault – we've been told enough times.
Who'd be a teacher? It just isn't rational
And now we must all teach the curriculum national;

Targets are set, and each child we'll test.
And teacher will know what to do with the rest.
Who'd be a teacher, when some half-witted pundit
Gets a half-witted theory, and half-wit to fund it.
Then duly announces 'Your methods are wrong:
Children learn best if you teach them in a song.'
Who'd be a teacher? We don't need more pay,
Just look at the length of our holiday:
And the hours aren't bad, nine until four;
So why aren't they queuing ten deep at the door?
Who'd be a teacher? Well I've no regret
That I'm leaving. I'm willing to make a small bet
There's a smidgen of envy in those remaining,
Who know in the future there'll be more complaining.
Who'd be a teacher; we all know the score;
Trials and frustrations we've all had, and much more.
But we've all felt the glow when a child has succeeded,
And the pride that we've helped to give what that child needed.
Who'd be a teacher? I'll make a confession,
I'm proud that I've been in this great profession.
And on this occasion I'll raise my glass -
'To teachers – God bless them – they're top of the class!'
      (Jennie Radley, former headteacher of Simms Cross County
      Infants School, Widnes. The poem is reproduced with kind
            permission of the *TES*)

So how can all staff be respected and recognised? Clearly, most of it has to come from within the school. First there is the planned visit by the headteacher to classrooms and departments; there is the seeking out of matters to praise, both by a handwritten note of thanks and by the spoken word. At staff meetings the wise leader will always seek to find ways of thanking colleagues by name for particular contributions. There is also the governors' meeting, where there is a need, for example, to ensure that the chair of governors seeks to praise the staff as well as the headteacher when there are public occasions.

It would be easy to elaborate on all the techniques for good management of interpersonal relationships. It is, after all, the one quality required above all others, as we imply in Chapter 2. It is certainly the key to staff development.

Set aside a time each day for thanking people.

People's personal needs require the most sensitive thought backed by a good system to make sure the thought is translated into action. You simply cannot leave to chance that you will regularly remember to have a word with a person and thank them. One of the best leaders we know used to set aside a quarter of an hour each day specifically for the purpose of writing notes to people about things she had observed that were good or that people had told her were good. Once the climate of positive reinforcement is established, it is that much easier to pick up on the occasional point of criticism, which is, of course, best done in private. Every now and then we will need that jolt too.

In successful schools, however, respect and recognition is not merely a 'top-down' process. It is particularly important among peer groups. So teachers can make their own lives more enjoyable simply by resolving to do things for each other. There is a social cement in staff rooms which is as intangible as it is real: it comes from shared social occasions.

> The teacher told me of the old days when they had gathered in each other's houses in the evenings, each bringing a dish or some drink and how they had stayed up to eleven, midnight or sometimes one in the morning, working on some scheme or other. You cannot legislate that but you can create a climate even in the wake of the pernicious 1,265 hours where it is more rather than less likely, where teachers will simply want to give much more time together.
>
> (New headteacher of a secondary school)

The final process of school improvement involves parents and the home and community curriculum.

The encouragement of parental and community involvement

The usual school lunchtime. The bell had sounded and there was the familiar accelerated pupil movement disgorging into a sunlit play-ground where games and conversations jostled in a good-humoured, boisterous dispute for space. Head and shoulders half inclined, the teacher was talking casually but seriously to the dishevelled 11- or 12-year-old boy who was looking anywhere but at the teacher. 'Trouble' was my suspicious and ungenerous thought as I stopped within earshot to look at the noticeboard. Closer hearing and a casual glance revealed that the boy was nodding and inspecting some object in the teacher's hand; with quick eye contact and a smile he took the object and disappeared.

The teacher was doing what good teachers do with early adoles-cents. She had brought in an early telescopic lens picked up for next to nothing in a junk shop with what we would call 'inclusive intent'. The teacher explained. She was finding Haroon as she put it, '. . . beyond me. I couldn't reach him, couldn't touch him. Nobody on the staff could. He is a loner . . . doesn't mix. Then I found out from an essay he wrote that he took photos. And when we went to the Indoor

35

Arena I got him to take some with my camera. Soon he was talking of his hobby: he collects old cameras, some working some not, collects old photos obsessively.'

Haroon was lucky. Well, all the pupils were at that school, for as one member of staff generously said, 'There's always something if you ask the right questions and between us – and that includes the lab assistants and the support staff – we do. There is usually one member of staff who can make a connection.' By 'making a connection' the teacher meant finding the means of showing the child that they were special to at least someone on the staff.

But the successful school goes much further. Just as the pupils suspend disbelief as a result of the unique and trusting relationship with the teacher in order that they can acquire a skill or understanding hitherto beyond their reach, so the wider local community knows when its school is going beyond what it strictly has to do. Local conversations illustrate a local community's approval and ambition. 'It is all right at such an' such a school,' they say to each other. 'They are always doing things for the kids.' 'Doing things for the kids' is shorthand for what many successful schools would recognise as a coherent set of interventions that, taken together, add up to their contribution to the home and community curriculum. In short, they go beyond the timetabled 15 per cent of time the pupils spend awake and in lessons and invade the 85 per cent which strictly speaking they do not need to occupy. Let us illustrate some of these interventions.

Homework

The regular setting and marking of relevant extension and reinforcement tasks of appropriate length. Clearly this will vary with the age of the child and the stage of learning, ranging from, for example, home–school reading pacts in infancy to the completion of GCSE coursework in Years 10 and 11. Schools are judged by the consistency of their homework practices, whether for example they are sustained throughout the year rather than simply for part of it. So the leadership of the school, whether as a whole or departmentally, reinforces homework consciousness by showing interest in it, even having prizes for it at awards evenings. Responsibility points are used for the staff who lead on homework. They know that by Key Stages 3 and 4 school-influenced homework can add between a quarter and a third to lesson time when account is taken of 'holiday tasks' too. In Key Stages 1 and 2 there is greater potential for using homework more overtly to promote the 'joint educator' role which is so necessary if

---

the parent is to be 'good enough'. The most advanced example we have seen of this comes from the Greenwood School in Nottingham with its graduated tasks for four days a week throughout Key Stage 2. Most of the tasks involve parent and child in necessarily joint activities.

Extra-curricular clubs and societies

The expectation is that committed members of staff – teachers and support staff alike – contribute in some way to extension, supplementary and enriching activities outside the formal school timetable. It is part of their professionalism. So chess clubs, dance and drama, debating, computers vie with each other on a menu that in a well-run school owes less to serendipity and more to a coherent recruitment and development policy for staff and pupils alike. Learning is not restricted to lessons.

Residentials

The value of the provision of a residential experience available to every pupil at least once during their primary and secondary education, as indicated in the Birmingham guarantees, should be part of what the school automatically offers to each and every child, not ski trips for the wealthy few. So the school monitors that each child in each of Key Stages 2, 3 and 4 has a week's residential for the sake of 'under canvas', 'environmental' and 'outdoor' challenge experiences.

Homework clubs

Secondary schools frequently offer an 'out-of-school-day' facility for children to find a place to do their homework where support, reference materials and resources are readily available in a quiet and purposeful atmosphere. (The Prince's Trust has, of course, to its great credit supported the creation and rapid expansion of such 'study support centres'.) In a school I visited recently Saturdays were available for Key Stage 3 pupils and Mondays to Thursdays for Key Stage 4.

School performances and sporting activities

Schools are places where there are opportunities within the sports and arts for youngsters to find their talent and give expression to it. School concerts, plays, musicals and sports teams flourish in the evenings and at weekends, often by deliberate linkages to local amateur clubs for adults, who see the links as lifeblood for their future health.

Holiday learning

Successful schools find ways to minimise the 'learning loss' through revision courses and summer holiday tasks set by teachers who will take the children in the upcoming year. Easter revision courses are an example of such development.

For the school to take stock of all these activities it needs to set them out as part of its vision, which necessarily needs to be shared with its partners in education, the parents or carers. Many schools do this less by the school prospectus, which has a marketing/consumer slant to it that may inhibit full understanding of the parental–educational partnership: they prefer instead to construct a home–school compact or understanding which sets out more clearly each side's responsibilities.

The key to these responsibilities it seems to us, is to be found in a small illustration of the practice glimpsed in one primary school recently. The head decided that parental consultations about pupil progress suffered from being scheduled in the middle of the school year when so much of the time in which the partners – parent and teacher – could do more in a concerted effort to improve the child's learning had already passed. Instead the school now starts the year with a discussion involving parent and teacher (and if necessary the previous year's teacher) in reviewing the completion of the pupil's summer holiday learning assignments, targets for learning experiences and outcomes for the forthcoming year. The home learning and experiences expected, for example spelling games, numeracy treasure hunts, family environmental projects, extended reading, video criticisms, and so on are also reviewed, together with a clear exposition of what will happen in school, including a review of extra-curricular activities and some anticipated pupil gains in skills and understandings. In this particular school all this became, in effect, a written individual learning plan for the year.

The school in question was doing this from Year 3 onwards and was planning to involve the pupils in the review in Years 5 and 6. The consequence has been that the subsequent mid-year parental consultation takes place with a more sharply focused debate of the contribution of each – pupil, teacher and parent – to the progress made. We know of no school, however, that has conducted this process for a sufficient length of time to be certain of its outcome in terms of measurable gains whether in attendance, academic attainment or behaviour. It is hard to believe, however, that the outcome of it all will be anything but positive. Of course it represents an example drawn from primary school practice, but it is easy to see that secondary schools could do something similar.

At the secondary level, however, any successful partnership which makes the best use of the home and community as well as the school and National Curriculum will require continuity of tutorial responsibility from year to year and a built-in faculty intention to measure subject progress by individual pupils from year to year. In this respect it may be sensible to focus on Key Stage 3 results as well as Key Stage 4 GCSE outcomes, at least in the core subjects. If this were done from the moment of the pupil's entry into the school it might be possible to catch the sense of accelerated progress (or at least minimise the likelihood of stalling) in the results obtained between the end of childhood at Key Stage 2 and during adolescence in Key Stages 3 and 4. After all, when we know that individuals can turn a modest level 3 at Key Stage 2 into a level 5 at Key Stage 3 and a Grade C at GCSE, we must be tantalised into realising that such success can be brought within the grasp of 80 per cent of the age group.

Set out elsewhere in this book is the need for home–school pacts or understandings. Such pacts (now enshrined in law and guidance to schools) provide the systemic framework for a meaningful relationship, but the wise school will seek to go beyond that and differentiate to meet the needs of different groups of parents. For instance, what will suit a school in the most rural areas is unlikely to be appropriate for an inner city where most parents are unemployed and either white fifth- or sixth-generation victims of the ebb tide of the revolutions in the industrial service sector or from the Asian sub-continent or elsewhere, speaking a different home language from the teachers and worshipping a different God, or the same one in a very different way.

The more open a school can be in its communication and receptiveness to different ways of doing things, the more likely it will be to enlist parental support.

Schools have become places where there are job opportunities for people with the right qualities but not necessarily with high-level qualifications, so jobs in the school meals service, in cleaning, as midday supervisors or classroom assistants have multiplied. Some headteachers have used the opportunity presented by these developments to recruit local parents to become support staff who themselves receive training on the job.

Sharon's story

It was a Friday afternoon in January. The mother's hands were shaking rather than trembling as she stood to read her account of what 'Schoolwise' meant to her. This is exactly what she read to a room where you could touch the silence among the sixty or so gathered there:

How my own experience influences how I am with children in class

Since having my children and being at home for 12 years I found I lost a lot of confidence in myself and thought my life was over. When my youngest started school I found it very hard to let her go as I felt I was the one left on my own. Then my children brought home the letter for Schoolwise course and my eldest son said 'You could do that, mum.' It made me feel good to think he still had faith in me. So I joined the course and met a lot of new friends but still felt I did not have confidence enough to join in. I was all right when we had to write things down and group work, but felt sick if I had to talk or ask questions on my own. The day I was going to pack in the course Carol came down with my homework and said Marie was looking for me and said my work was excellent. I didn't believe it until I read what she had written on the end of it. I was so pleased with myself for the first time in a long time. I danced around the house, kept reading the comment and feeling great. I decided not to give up the course as I feel my confidence in myself is coming back slowly. It has taught me not to give up on myself so easy, as if I keep trying hard enough I can probably get on. When I am in the classroom and see a child who hasn't got a lot of confidence, I go and see what's wrong. I try and help the best I can if they are not sure what to do or don't understand what has to be done. I try and explain in a way they understand.

I also find praise can go a long way and make you feel great. So I praise the children where praise is needed and let them know they can try anything. It doesn't matter if it is right all the time as they can learn a lot from their mistakes.

You can imagine why she received rapturous applause as she sat down. Here was a parent rediscovering the joy of learning and through it the confidence to contribute to others' learning. It made me think.

Sharon's story – I have given her a pseudonym – arises from 'Schoolwise', based at East Birmingham College of Further Education and on the leadership of a magical lecturer there, Joy Warmington. The scheme (or course, as it has to be called to qualify for Further Education Funding Council funding) is based on the assumption that by linking the process of volunteering to adult learning it is possible to prompt learning among adults, particularly parents, in the community, with their local schools. It's a case of getting double value or using time twice.

Sharon herself represents thousands of parents, especially mothers, in

Birmingham. The last of their children is about to start nursery or primary school – some keep the last-born away from nursery because they want their child's company. One headteacher told me the other day that she makes a point of knowing and inviting in for a social get-together – she's that sort of head-teacher – those mothers who are sending the youngest to school the following year so that they can share their worries, which turn out to be very similar to Sharon's. She calls it her 'last-born parents' group. She then links them up with Schoolwise. Sharon's story made me think of other parent initiatives across the city. 'Parentwise', for example, is very similar and owes a great deal to North Birmingham College. Then there were the amazing celebrations in Sparkbrook and Sparkhill last November, when 200 parents were acknowledged enthusiastically for their learning. All had been ensnared into learning through their concern for their children's schooling and all endorsed Sharon's words. Their particular scheme had owed a great deal to South Birmingham College, the Basic Skills Agency, the Family Literacy Initiative and a local energy creator who worked between the school and the college and among the parents. There are countless other examples: work in Kings Norton, especially the early learning scheme for first-time parents, workers in Northfield and Longbridge, both in individual schools and in co-operation with Bournville College and the city's adult education service.

There is no doubt that the funding methods of the Further Education Funding Council, coupled with the availability of other grants, have enabled some schools to forge impressive network arrangements with colleges of further education to provide a sudden and immediately available treasure trove of further training for their parents in family literacy or basic and extended skills courses.

A teacher's teacher

She was a remarkable teacher by any standard. In a sense she was a teacher's teacher. Let me explain. I came across her briefly in one of our primary schools, late one afternoon recently, when many are winding down for the end of the school day.

Ends of lessons and ends of days are a much debated issue in school staffrooms where teaching and learning are taken seriously.

For this young woman, who had reached that confident stage of expertise and energy which comes after the initial phase of teaching, it was a chance to cram yet more in. The class was brought effortlessly and willingly together – they responded to her every look – and the tape recorder was set running, to the delight of her Year 5 pupils. Unobtrusively, with a conspiratorial glance which was silently and smilingly acknowledged by the miscreant who was fiddling with it in abstracted concentration while his mind was elsewhere, she delicately removed the pencilholder from a nearby table.

The rest of the class were too busy listening to notice. The whole class was in rapt attention to the peer group's tape work. The group's task seemed to have involved researching the first moon landing and then creating a tape 'faction', in this case their own series of interviews, with other pupils taking on the roles of the famous astronauts.

The teacher raised her hand. At the sign, the child depressed the stop button. There then followed the most persistent, almost contagiously irresistible, quick-fire questioning of the group who had created the tape to that point. Discussion of fact and opinion about possible courses of action which had led to the trip and about the trip itself bounced and flowed around the classroom and from her inspired teaching members of other groups – there had clearly been more than one group – joined in as spokespersons for their colleagues' discoveries.

Her hand was raised once more and the tape restarted. We were into the next piece of the programme, put together by another group, those in charge of ground control for the space exploration. But then, just as it had started, her hand was up again. 'I am sorry Class 5,' she said, 'it's the end of the day, it's time to go home.' There was a groan of collective disappointment, quickly assuaged by her look. 'Tomorrow', she declared predictably, 'we will have episodes 2, 3 and 4. We will start a little earlier if we all get our discovery done. We must get through the whole piece by the end of the week . . . maybe we will miss afternoon break.' 'Yes Miss, let's,' came more than one voice.

What is special about this teacher in one of our inner-city schools, where there are high levels of poverty and disadvantage? Make no mistake about it, she walks with genius. That is why I say she is a teacher's teacher. Just as top golfers, tennis players, cricketers, footballers, practitioners in all sports, can tell you appreciatively of outstanding talent among their colleagues, so too can teachers. The difference is, of course, that leading sports people receive a king's ransom in wages and wide public acclaim – even adoration – while the superteacher has to make do with an anonymous life. If Eric Cantona is worth £10,000 a week, the teacher I saw in Small Heath is worth twice that amount.

There was a pace and urgency about the teacher's mind and a calmness about her movement which was a formidable combination. You see it sometimes when visiting primary classrooms. It is not so much that such teachers resent your visits, rather that they see you as a possible further resource for learning, or as a spectator who will soon see the urgency of the business in hand. It was quite simply as good an end to a school day as I have ever seen. Indeed, ends of lessons and end of school days, as I have remarked earlier, are a topic worth debating in their own right. A respected junior school colleague of mine of many years standing tells me that she always indulges her interest in enthralling stories: 'It lures them on, you see, wherever they are with their reading development,' she declares. 'I have a lot of old favourites, and many new ones with the expansion of high quality children's literature these days, which I doctor to make sure the pace is urgent and the vocabulary mind-stretching on occasion, within a story which is magnetic.' She went on: 'So long as *you* end each day's episode on a point of suspense, that is the vital bit. Then you reduce any chance of absenteeism. They cannot wait to hear the next bit and of course sometimes the class choose their alternative endings.'

Maurice Galton, who conducted the Oracle (Observational Research and Classroom Learning Evaluation) study of late junior and early secondary teaching practices a decade or more ago, still speaks of an outstanding practitioner who defies his analysis. 'She practises a kind of studied unpredictability in her teaching' he confided to me not long ago. Apparently she even used the children's dismissal at the end of a lesson, setting the whole class to debate the criteria to be used as each 'table' left the room. For her class, ends of lessons were a medley of mental arithmetic one week, vocabulary games the next and going 'joyously', 'sadly' or 'seriously-and-worriedly' the next.

School life for her pupils, as it was for those in the class of my young friend in Small Heath, is one long, unpredictable and stimulating journey of discovery and learning. The pupils do not know yet – they will one day of course – that they are privileged to be taught by a Leonardo da Vinci or a Michelangelo of our profession. We need to know more about such teachers – what makes them tick, what they do that makes other teachers respect them. That is why the National Primary Centre's recently announced invitation to schools and teachers to nominate examples of interesting practice for an award scheme is so welcome. It is time we celebrated our outstanding colleagues: we can learn so much from them.

2

LEADERSHIP

All the research confirmed by HMI and more recently, OFSTED, suggests that leadership in schools is *the* key factor in improvement and success. Our studies – and the example of Birmingham schools which have changed most in one direction or another – support that theory. And yet our contention is that leadership is extremely complex: it is simply not enough to say profoundly 'it is all down to the headteacher' as though one is speaking a self-evident truth and, with a shrug, affecting the inevitability and certainty of truth, walk away.

First of all leadership is not all down to the headteacher, the head of department or, in the classroom, the teacher. If it is, nobody is learning anything at all about leadership. The first rule about leadership is that it is shared.

The first rule of leadership is that it is shared

In the classroom, the teacher, even of the youngest infants, shares leadership between herself and learning assistant, not on some strict 'You do this, I do that' basis but with a deliberate sharing of information about learning, about activities to be jointly planned and then jointly carried out. Monitoring of whole lessons, child observations or test results are all partly the responsibility of learning assistants in some of our schools. In one of our schools, reading progress is a joint responsibility of the English co-ordinator and the learning assistant deputed to give whole-school support to the work of the co-ordinator in addition to her classroom duties.

Nor does it stop there. We were visited by Gerry Freiberg from Texas and our schools were enthralled by his exposition on 'pupil leadership' which is enabled by all teachers. As a result we have seen many examples of classrooms where pupil monitoring jobs are advertised and applications sought from the whole class against clearly defined job descriptions which incorporate work and responsibility for leading on a particular issue – for example, supporting ways in which the room might be better organised. Once appointed to the job the successful pupil applicant has targets associated with those duties for the year, as well as targets for their learning. Of course, the smaller the school or teaching unit, the more leadership, as well as work, can be shared.

The co-ordinator of English in the primary school needs time to exercise management tasks in order that leadership can be linked to reality rather than wishful thinking. So unless the co-ordinator has time to carry out the constructive and supportive shaping, coaching, questioning of all practitioners of English alongside them in classrooms, the effect will be minimal. Like all leaders, the co-ordinator is thinking strategically as they do the job. After all, most of us do at least two or three things at once. In a field for which we are responsible as leaders we have thought about strategy, about great leaps forward through modified action all the time – in the car, on the radio, in conversations and if not exactly as we teach, immediately afterwards in the spoken recollection of the lesson. In the area in which we lead, those whom we lead for that purpose expect us to have long-sightedness and a wider field of vision. If we haven't but pretend we do, we immediately lose legitimacy as leaders.

Leaders need long-sightedness and a wider field of vision.

If we are clever, we learn all the time from others, both from their mistakes and from their infectious successes. So a language co-ordinator does not need time in school to plan, to analyse, to mark, to write the next paper: they do that out of school when the children have gone home. In school they do what they can only do when lessons are on, when children are learning, when teachers are teaching: coaching by working alongside, observing interchanges and the use of materials. They ask questions and speculate. They practise teaching and learning, commenting on the amount and impact of paired reading going on in Year 6 as well as Year 2, observing the use of the puppet dolls in the sharing of language, the expansion of vocabulary as children progress up the school with targets set and targets analysed. They celebrate the class teacher who uses the end-of-day storytime to teach rather than to amuse, at home they write up all that they see for a staff debate, and they enable all staff to observe each other doing paired work or storytime at the end of the day.

So that is how the language co-ordinator uses their 'non contact-time'.

Exactly the same applies to the head of department in a secondary school. In one of our schools the head of department uses every one of his 'free' periods in other colleagues' lessons. An analysis of his seven 'free' periods reveals regular teaching alongside the newly qualified teacher (one lesson a week with different groups throughout the first term: 'it enabled me to talk with her after school, not just about that group, but about her approaches generally: questioning technique, her own behaviour, pace, ends of lessons that sort of thing'). For one lesson he 'springs free' each of his colleagues in turn so that they can observe each other in the context of a paper on teachers of good science teaching 'which we hope to publish'; two lessons he spends working with the laboratory learning assistants on preparation, generally listening, seeing what needs to be ordered, how they see their new young colleague 'settling in', and the rest of the time he spends in the library working with individual children, mentoring them and some of his own tutor groups in science.

What do we learn from these two leaders at classroom and departmental level? They are doing what industrial managers would call 'walking the job' or 'sticking close to the knitting'. Neither claim to do what we have described every week throughout the year. Both say it is possible to keep it up in the autumn term but that once life becomes hectic around Christmas and later in the year other priorities and crises take over. But they see that as a bit of a defeat and are debating how to overcome it. Maybe their targets are too ambitious.

Both respect their headteachers and their actions, interest, words and support. So, for example, there is no question of the language co-ordinator or the head of science covering 'an absent colleague in the first ten weeks of the autumn term', although it is an accepted practice in term two. Where is the headteacher in all this? What each case appears to show is a self-motivated co-ordinator and an autonomous head of department exercising leadership. Drop in on their staff meetings or look at their policy documents and you will find that each and every member of staff teaching English in the primary school or science in the secondary school is leading 'on some aspect of development'.

As it happens, the headteacher is involved in this aspect of leadership too. In both cases the headteachers take part in curriculum debate and in teaching and learning discussions. In the primary case it was by sharing a planning session and doing some phonic work with a small group in each year group's classroom (comprising only two 30-minute sessions in a week, but both carefully structured and planned). Moreover, the head prepared a joint paper with the language co-ordinator for a staff meeting discussion. In the case of the science department, the head and two deputies took over the teaching of science, again on a prepared and planned basis, on two Thursdays in the spring term and then joined a science department meeting to review their targets for improved performance at Key Stage 3 and in GCSE.

What these leaders – heads, or heads of department, or curriculum co-ordinators, or teachers – are seen to do, what they show interest in, how they notice effort, commitment and quality, all vitally affects their schools. The point we are trying to make, however, is that if we focus too much on the headteacher's role in leadership there is a great danger we shall neglect the way in which the leader of the school themself doesn't seek to hog the limelight or, as Michael Fullan set out in an unpublished monograph, 'blind others with their vision'. We have already hinted at the complexity of the issue, though we do think the headteacher's role in the school is 'key', so we have a very clear view about how and paradoxicallly successful headteachers spend their time, what they say, how they say it, what time they give to their constituents – all staff, all parents, all pupils, as well as a wider community of, for example, business – and it is mainly with the headteacher in mind that we have written this chapter.

Leadership, therefore, in successful schools is not seen as the exclusive quality of one person. One person may be 'key' but leadership is shared – among pupils, teachers and other staff and members of the community.

Pupils as leaders

Each year teacher educators commission students in training to carry out classroom observation of a particular child and to construct and research a sociogram of the activity among certain pupils. In the classroom setting children acknowledge leaders of two kinds: those whom they fear and those whom they like. The influence of those they fear – the bully or the would-be bully – is reluctant: it is as though the 'disliked' leader is the north pole of a magnet pushing against another north pole which retreats or twitches from one side to the other to try to avoid contact. Successful teachers know all about that. They also recognise in each of their classes those whom the rest of the class acknowledge as unofficial leaders. They debate in staffrooms the various strategies they deploy to enlist potential disruptives. They try giving them jobs to do, special tasks to perform, before resorting to extreme measures. Indeed, one of the features of the everyday practice of good teachers is the way they share out tasks and leadership among members of their classes.

So it is among staff.

Teachers as leaders

Over a period stories stick to successful leaders: they are laced with a potent mixture of affection and – usually but not always – amused respect. Such people are magnets to myths and legends. The stories, of course, often grow with the telling but their influence on newcomers is great.

So it is that the adult can recall from their school days a 'character' among their teachers:

> She was an absolute dragon – mind you, she made you want to work,

or,

> He was weird – always wore a yellow jacket with his shirt hanging out, but he didn't half get us to learn.

It is still true in schools that the teachers who have the most influence on children's motivation, learning and development, are those with whom they have a worthwhile relationship. They are interested and interesting. They are the *real* leaders in the everyday business of schooling.

Ask a group of children, if you can, the school teachers to whom they relate well and tot up the outcome. There you will have a league table of people who exercise leadership in the classroom. One of us who carried out such an exercise in a school of 630 pupils with which we were working found that one teacher attracted an astonishing 450 nominations. Such teachers are much more likely to create the 'magic moments' of schooling: those moments when the learners realise the feeling of having been stretched and energised, when they are doing something that they thought they wouldn't be able to achieve or understanding an issue which beforehand they were sure was beyond their comprehension.

Such leaders are developers of other people's skills, actions and beliefs. For good and ill, they can also act as 'unofficial leaders' amongst the staff. The member of staff without paid responsibility to whom the rest of the staff defer during (and, most significantly, outside) staff meetings is a leader. Amongst teaching staff the colleague who is enormously committed to children and school life and whom others know, via the grapevine, that the pupils' respect is a touchstone for collective decisions.

There are also equivalents in the staffroom of the classroom bully. They hold sway at dark moments when the whole system is in danger of falling apart. People seek to avoid their company but those in official positions of leadership know that at moments of crisis their influence can be critical.

> I remember a particularly harrowing occasion. We'd had bad publicity in the local paper . . . I knew the staff meeting would be tense and could go either way . . . So I spoke to Jim Mackay – technology teacher and a trouble maker. It was in the lunch hour . . . . we both watch soccer at Maine Road . . . asked him to come to see me after school about the away match . . . It was just enough . . . he remained quiet.
>
> Headteacher's conversation

Potential leadership: expanding the supply of energy

In the setting of the school, the wise leader analyses the exercise of leadership as it is and as it might become. There are leaders amongst all the various stake-holders of the school – governors, teaching staff, support staff, parents, pupils, local business people. They are of at least the two sorts we have already described, those who are feared and those who are liked.

One school we know is genuinely trying to share leadership amongst the whole-school community. It has started by carrying out sociograms amongst the pupils – using teachers in training to do it – in order to identify and develop as a strategy the potential leadership qualities of those that others in the class regard as leaders. In the process it is discovering the 'north pole–north pole' leaders and finding in a simultaneous survey of bullying an uncanny over-lap of individuals. Interestingly, too, it finds among some of those in the 'north pole–north pole' category of leaders a very high general intelligence score. They represent essentially unrealised talent. It has ushered in a debate about the appropriateness of the curriculum, both in school and out of school, for those particular pupils.

In order to capitalise on sharing opportunities for leadership, the school is also making an inventory of essential tasks and possible additional opportunities for leadership. The school is being careful not to confuse *work* with *responsibility* in analysing leadership. Most people in employment, as we have seen, find that they have too much of the former and not enough of the latter. Harnessing potential leadership is a way of increasing the supply of energy available to everyone.

Healthy schools and their teachers know 'their work is never done'. There is always the chance that if one put in a little bit more time with that youngster in Year 9 or Year 3, there would be a chance that one would unlock the talent which is the school's main goal.

> I decided to lay on an extra maths club because I thought it might appeal to Wayne in 8J and John and Lisa in 9S and those three boys in Ann Jones's class in the first year. I knew that I could get John and Lisa involved, because of the way that they looked at each other in class. And there were the other two in Year 10. But what I really hoped for was that in an 'interest-led' mixed age group, all the particular needs of Tony could be sorted – and he is a good lad and really could take off. He has just got this barrier in his mind about maths: it is all confidence really. And I don't get enough time with him, he is too worried about what his mates might think.
>
> (Head of Maths)

The work, like the responsibility, has to be shared. Unless the responsibility is shared, however, the bank account of credit in work will soon run dry. People feel they don't matter. They haven't got a stake in where the school is going. That is what is so worrying about the cumulative overloading effects of the National Curriculum and its assessment arrangements.

> So I knew that Ann Jones – that is the teacher of Year 7 – I knew that she was ready to develop. It is her second year in teaching so I asked her what she thought about extra-curricular clubs. She jumped at it – said she could remember in her school how much she enjoyed hockey and such. What if we could really transform the kids' approach to maths – so they could regard it as being fun? She was away after that. Couldn't stop her. Not only has she started the maths – and I gave up two lunch times to help – but she has influenced young Sandy Kerr – he is the new historian and he has started a club. But the clever thing about Ann – I would never have thought of it myself – is the way she has got the pupils taking responsibility

for the club themselves. They produced a news sheet. Sometimes I think we wouldn't need to be there because they are helping each other as much as we are helping them. We are all running a family maths day soon.

(Head of Maths)

In exploiting the rich talent of leadership in the school community, successful leaders like this head of maths have faced squarely the lack of sufficient resources, time and staff and have avoided the 'if only . . .' syndrome of transferring the blame to forces outside their control. They have decided they will do a lot more of the extra work needed.

You can guesss the implication of what we have said about the limitation of 'pushing' in the 'north pole–north pole' model of leadership wherever it occurs – in the classroom, the staffroom or amongst senior management. Top-down and directive leadership gets from staff their contractual obligations and nothing more. On the other hand, we see advantages in the 'north pole–south pole' leadership style in the school, especially in headteachers. If it is the case that driven staff will do only what they have to do, the magnetic qualities of opposites can unlock enormous surges of energy and effort among professionals. And yet that model too is limited:

The head is charismatic, certainly, but he crowds the rest of us out. He casts such a big shadow. It all depends on him. There's no doubting his commitment – and we all work hard for him . . . but I wish he would let others take the lead.

(Senior teacher)

Indeed, a survey of teacher attitudes conducted by Keele University showed that the one thing teachers regret in notions of leadership is any feeling of being 'followers'. They are, after all, professionals making decisions in every lesson in a way which they know affects the real business of the school, the learning and development of the pupils. Teachers know they make the vital decisions. In a sense they know they are the people who are really leading by example, so they look for certain qualities in their leaders – heads of departments, post holders with responsibility allowances, deputies and headteachers. They need to respect such people.

Values: the importance of leaders' behaviour

All we can say about the values of the schools which seem to us to be successful, is that their values are not those of the market place: they are not preoccupied with 'getting one over' on competitor schools, but are simply determined not to be undermined by them. They show genuine concern for the work of all the staff, not just some. There seems to be a real commitment to celebrating the achievements of all pupils rather than a few. Although the leaders themselves don't mention it, those who like and respect their leaders talk of their 'idealism', their 'integrity', the 'trust she puts in you and you respond', their sense of humour, which can range from the quiet to the outlandish but always includes an element of self-mockery, and their ability to convince those outside the school of the confident pride in all that the school community achieves, together with its restless determination and expectation to achieve more, rather than sit back on its laurels. These qualities can be readily seen and recognised with certainty by others. Rarely, however, are they obvious when somebody first assumes a position of leadership There might be promising signs but everybody will know that the proof of the pudding will lie in their actions. Especially convincing to staff is commitment, evidenced by time and energy given to the task.

Particularly impressive was one female head who confessed to us that until she became head, she had had no interest in any kind of sport:

> 'But I knew it was important for lots of people and also believed that exercise was essential to a healthy approach to life. And of course it is important to most children, particularly at a certain age when they fantasise about being sporting heroes. So I make most of my assemblies rest on sporting stories and I call on pupils and staff alike to give accounts in assemblies of the school's successes. I have even learnt the rules of football and cricket, and', she ended with a smile, 'do you know, I even attended my first test match with a party from the school and I must admit I really enjoyed it. I learnt so much and now there is one other joy in life.'

> (Female headteacher)

This particular head is an enthusiast for music. She has an impressive voice and a range of interests from classic to contemporary pop and takes part, bewilderingly, in both a madrigal and a pop-singing group which the youngsters run in the lunch break. Music is blooming as the pupils see her interests translated into participation.

Another head we know is a saxophone player given to versification. Staff meetings, parents' evenings, awards' occasions, even the introduction of government initiatives are made memorable and the staffroom is full of erudite, witty, mocking ditties, limericks and verses. The examples amongst leaders are legion. Among our group is a weightlifter, an environmentalist who is reshaping not merely the grounds but the whole local community, an outdoor pursuits enthusiast and numerous sports people. There is even one poet.

What each of these 'freaks' does — for they are freaks in a way, slightly oddball, exceptionally unselfconscious in their fads and interests — what each does is to work out how to ensure that the school doesn't in consequence become lopsided. They are certainly magnetic to the younger generation, whose behaviour, attitudes and pastimes are shaped into some purposeful interest as a consequence. Ideally, there emerges a kaleidoscope of interests as other members of staff feel it legitimate to exhibit their particular interests too. One staff-room traced it all back to an 'activity week' when the timetable had been suspended and suddenly everybody's real interests had been revealed and celebrated.

> I understand and sympathise in a way with the government's idea of specialism. We are really quite exceptional in music and it is true to say we aren't in technology – well at least not at design and making things, we are not bad on the basic skills. These things wax and wane. I accept, I suppose, I have never let the music go, but there is no reason why, with the new appointment coming up in CDT, we shouldn't suddenly blossom there. I will be looking for that in the appointment and I will earmark large chunks in my diary to give every possible encouragement to see the new person, whoever he or she is, succeed. I want us to excel at everything.
>
> (Headteacher)

So if the values of the leader are seen in their actions, are there any common base values we share that inform the schools? We noted by implication 'inclusive' actions – the wish to enlist or 'bring on side' as many people in the community as possible. Aided schools refer to the strength they draw from being overtly religious in character:

> Don't get me wrong. Teachers don't have to be Christian. It's just up front that the school is Christian in foundation so they need to be comfortable with that . . . In fact we have Sikhs, Hindus and Moslems in abundance . . . It's more an unspoken assumption about honesty and integrity in our dealings, valuing all talents – we have a special unit for the visually impaired for example.
>
> (Deputy head)

Certainly the leaders most respected in the schools we had pointed out to us as successful were people who understood the considerably differing expectations of the different principal client groups – the pupils, the staff and the parents – and knew who they were and simply acted on that certainty.

It is in the way that they are talked about in day-to-day activities that values are established. They may be formally articulated in a statement of school aims or in speeches to parents and in assemblies. These articulations are necessary but valueless, even damaging, if they are not demonstrated in the care and integrity with which the leader approaches their task. People will hear the fine statement of objectives and – values – the mission statement, if one can still stand this overworked phrase. But they will not do much about it until they see it in practice and feel it pervading the management actions of the school.

Watching successful heads in action one realises that they work in very different ways and run very different schools. What unites them is that they are men and women with ideals and the ability to share those ideals with those whom they lead. They might cavil at the description but our observation is that, to the best of their ability, they live their ideals: in the way they answer a colleague who comes to the door, the exchange with a pupil in the corridor, the response to their secretary. In minute ways they build up an ethos. They need to sell the ideals as well, indeed to keep restating them, but it is the daily attention to the details which wins the day.

Are there then some ideal values which all heads should be propagating? Uniformity is not what is wanted; different schools and their environments call for different values. Nonetheless, there do appear to be some common themes which need to be there even if in varied forms. A commitment to the full development of every child, the pursuit of quality, the development of awareness of others: all those are universal.

That would be the first clarification for heads to take on board. Everything matters, not for what you do but for the way in which you do it. At the end of the day what you will have achieved is not answering a stack of letters, some problems solved and some people seen. Those will indeed have passed on their way but they are ephemeral. The little bit that you have contributed to building and cementing your school's values is what will last, together, of course, with the bit of you that you will never know about, which has rubbed off on other people.

We all need to feel we are doing something worthwhile. That is what gives meaning to our lives and stimulates us to work hard, a fact which one can observe in the staffrooms of all the schools we work in. There are hundreds of dedicated teachers who work really hard for their ideals of service to children. It is the job of management to bring those ideals together into a common set of objectives. Then everyone will be reinforced by their awareness of working in a team. Maybe the focus will help individuals to be even more effective. Certainly, praise and recognition will have that result.

Is it right to give this recognition by saying 'thank you'? This sometimes seems patronising, as if the school's success were the personal fief of the head or whoever is saying thank you. We need to make clear our warm enthusiasm for the work everyone does to further the values for which we all stand. In short, the enthusiasm needs to be linked not just to the measure of work put in but to the shared higher purpose of the school. Thank yous should be private and personal as well as public and collective; they should vary and be unpredictable. Above all they should demonstrate a celebration of success and achievement in the ultimate value of the school and the department, for in this way a school or department accumulates its history, extending the run of recent and long-treasured successes.

A key ingredient to school success is the extent to which the values of school life are shared among all the members of the community. Life outside may be very different, but in school there is a code of conduct and of behaviour which all try to sustain in their dealings with each other and the outside world.

Underpinning the values there are two preliminary qualities of behaviour which improve the chances of success in leadership. They are not restricted to individuals but can inform practice from classrooms through the corridors to the headteacher's office.

Be cheerful and optimistic

This varies from simple things such as bothering to say a cheerful 'good morning' rather than offering a preoccupied stare, to a more considered set of strategies to find the humour in crisis. It is to avoid the classic story told to me by one colleague about the first day of term in a large secondary school, when the head, in all seriousness, said to the assembled staff, 'Now I know that there is nowhere we would less like to be this morning than here.'

Even if the leader feels it – and if he or she really and regularly does, there is probably an alarm bell warning him or her that it is time to go – there is absolutely no need to mention it. One American once said that unwarranted optimism was the real key to leadership, and a momentary reflection on the apparently irresolvable crisis of school life confirms it. How often has a teacher, on being told of a calamity and asked what to do, cheerfully told people to be calm and that there was no problem, when internally they were asking themselves what on earth they were to do!

Most people expect their leaders to see more of the total scene than they individually can do, so a lack of optimism insidiously undermines their morale. In a sense, leaders need vision and those who accompany them need to feel that they have seen the other side of the mountain. If leaders are pessimistic and then show it to others, there is clearly a problem in the longer vision leaders are tacitly credited with possessing.

Be welcoming and ready to be enthusiastic

To remain seated or even to stand behind a desk which faces the door, is not welcoming to visitors. So attention to the quality, use and disposition of furniture helps, as does the entrance to the school. The successful leader sees the need for welcome in many aspects of school life: in the room arrangement, the entrance foyer. Not for them the bleak double doors with those messages to report to an office, the whereabouts of which is not immediately obvious. The idea of 'welcome' informs every detail of the administration of the school, from signposts and notices to staff handbooks.

It is apparent too in the process of appointments, from the interview for the new post to a proper induction programme for all staff, not just teachers. There will be a booklet as a guide for occasional supply teachers, whose comparative views of schools in a locality can be a very telling messenger. It is manifest – or not – in the treatment of students in training when they are on practice. In any organisation the value of the smile in the reception area, whether from pupils as part of a rota or from staff, is crucial.

Genuine enthusiasm is infectious but more than simply a gift.

The head of department whose concern is to optimise the style and contribution of colleagues is evident in the welcoming of new ideas, even if some are known to be largely impractical. 'We don't do things that way here' is a comment that has its place, but only rarely. Newcomers can often see things which longer serving colleagues have long since ceased to notice. We noted one headteacher who asked all new members of staff to tell her after six months what were the three best features of the school and what were the three worst, and why. In many of the classrooms we visited the teachers had set an example for the rest of the school in the warmth of the surroundings which greeted their pupils in every lesson they experienced there.

Enthusiasm was transmitted in at least some of our schools by a shared determination to find things to praise.

> We start every staff briefing with some sort of congratulation. It's not forced. It's the same in department meetings. It comes from everyone
> (Probationer)

At the heart of successful leadership is a more than passing competence in three processes or skills, namely delegation, time management and the management of change.

Delegation

At the best of times delegation is a skill which most people in management find difficult. It is all the more so in teaching and in schools where one of the prevailing themes is generosity – the willingness to walk the extra mile on behalf of somebody – and where the whole belief system is founded on a commitment far beyond the call of duty. In our conversations with nearly 500 teachers we found only three enthusiasts for performance related pay. So you want people to volunteer for residential trips with Year 7 youngsters, you need them to take on a whole host of extra-curricular activities. You want them to feel obligated to people, especially the children in their charge. They are hardly likely to retain such values and generosity if they are paid on a different basis. Nevertheless, there is a downside to those values and characteristics. People who have made their career in that environment find it more than usually difficult to strike the right balance of delegation. One of our heads reminded us that:

> Although the buck stops here, it doesn't mean I have to confuse the arrival of the buck with carrying it all the time.
>
> (Headteacher)

Indeed, if you act as the hero or heroine leader, you literally collapse under the strain of all the tasks as well as the responsibilities which people heap on you.

Frequently, headteachers express surprise to each other about the sort of detail which a mutual acquaintance gets into when dealing with a particular issue, say the finance of the school. They experience uncomfortable reassurance by congratulating each other that they don't regard that particular activity as important and that old so-and-so can't be doing the right thing. The reassurance can never be total because, at a time of great change which is externally imposed, there is the ever-present worry that something of immense importance is happening or that the implications of such and such an initiative, if appreciated, could in a lateral way solve a perennial problem of the schools in which they are heads. Our experience of heads and their use of time and their adoption of particular priorities is that their choice of time and task varies and the practice of delegation varies accordingly. There is no single right answer.

One headteacher's enormous interest in finance and organisation is for another of our case studies simply a waste of time. They rely on their deputy, or in quite a few cases a well-paid bursar who is a member of the senior management team, to do all the finance. Delegation in matters financial is for Ann almost total. All she seems to worry about is to make priority decisions at budget-making time; she leaves budget management entirely to others. John however, another of our heads, sees the monitoring of spending patterns as a time-consuming but worthwhile priority: he would see it as a key to all sorts of possible initiatives and changes. We do not make judgements on these issues: we make the point that the principles of delegation are important. We came across an invaluable aid to managers/leaders in the difficult issue of delegation, reproduced on p. 58.

We know this scheme came from Cheshire and believe it has its origins in their comparative management work with industry and commerce. From what we have already said, it is clear that different heads have different preferred delegation positions in respect of particular aspects of school work. That, as we have implied, is legitimate. What is not so obvious, and requires some careful thought, is whether your perception of where you are over a particular issue is shared by those to whom you are delegating. It is clear that you will have preferences to be either at the top or at the bottom of the scale, but in respect of a particular task or a particular individual you will vary from time to time. A recipe for disaster is for either party to have a different perception of where that particular position is. At one school we know people actually carry the chart around with them and agree that they will remind each other on every occasion where they think they are on the scale of points 1 to 9.

Delegation: the Cheshire scheme

1 Look into this problem. Give me all the facts. I will decide what to do.
2 Let me know the alternatives available with the pros and cons of each. I will decide which to select.
3 Let me know the criteria for your recommendation, which alternatives you have identified, and which one appears best to you with any risks identified. I will make the decision.
4 Recommend a course of action for my approval.
5 Let me know what you intend to do. Delay action until I approve.
6 Let me know what you intend to do. Do it unless I say not to.
7 Take action. Let me know what you did. Let me know how it turns out.
8 Take action. Communicate with me only if your action is unsuccessful.
9 Take action. No further communication with me is necessary.

Of course, it is never as hard and fast as the list implies, even on a particular occasion. The skilful or enabling headteacher or department manager will encourage colleagues' behaviour to move closer and closer to the bottom half rather than the top half of the list, in order to share leadership and develop their colleagues' talents.

Time management

We remarked at the outset that we were impressed by the enviable ability of some leaders and managers effectively to use time twice. While they do one thing, they take the opportunity of doing another. At its simplest, the teacher in the classroom demonstrates this facility when walking around from group to group in a science laboratory whilst completing simple maintenance to planning tasks en route. In schools we know almost everyone seems to work very hard, so to pick out examples of heads of department or heads using time twice is not signalling that they work hard. They are simply being more effective at getting things done. In the main, for example, headteachers don't have time to mark work properly – another reason why heads should examine their own need to teach. Frequently they are forced to do it and forget that the preparation and follow-up time is the vital time they have not budgeted for.

Not only do successful leaders apparently have more time available than anyone else, they also convey a timelessness even when they are pressed. Some people, given an important engagement – a public speech of some sort, with the need to produce a paper – organise their diaries to give themselves 'time to think' and prepare: they build cushions before and after the event. Other leaders simply seem to pick it up on the wing, 'speak off the top of their head' and with a charge of adrenaline, perform outstandingly well. If any teacher, however, were to reflect how, after ten years, they know they could teach any lesson in their subject to almost any group, at a moment's notice, they would be less surprised by the ability of experienced headteachers and leaders to perform to large audiences at will. Just as the teacher's preparation lies in thousands of lessons, meticulously prepared and practised, so the head has a storehouse of possible speeches available and can merely orchestrate the appropriate thoughts and elements, confident in their basic materials. Moreover, the audiences are often composed of groups who are unknown to each other in such a context, so that there is a readiness to accept most things, providing the tone and the length is right. The more experienced the leader, the more the disposition of time changes, so new heads will need more time for speech preparation than those with more experience. Moreover, new heads need to spend as much time as possible with their main constituents – teachers, support staff, governors, parents, local primary heads (if a secondary school), pre-school agencies (if a primary school). The larger the area of responsibility, the more numerous the constituents and the more work and time is required.

After three or four years – after induction is over – the mutual confidence is such that leaders can spend less time assiduously cultivating relationships. They are established, although they need topping up and every so often with intensive attention. The grapevine will always be warning leaders about this person or that group in need of some special attention or another. That is where close colleagues are invaluable: they alert you to that need.

We have already referred to the need to 'use time twice', and there is a link between management and the management of change. It is the practice of 'piggybacking'. In managing change, one of the distinguishing features of those who seem to handle it most successfully is that they harness an *external imperative,* for example the introduction of some aspect of the National Curriculum, with an *internal collective need,* for example galvanising a science department, on top of an *individual wish,* for example the capacity of the second in the science department to exercise leadership.

The management of change

Twenty years ago there was no need for a headteacher or a head of department to understand much about the management of change. That, immediately, is an incorrect statement in the sense that all worthwhile and successful schools

59

have always generated change in curriculum approaches from within. Nevertheless, it is interesting that HMI in their review of leadership qualities in 1988 included for the first time as an essential ingredient in successful schooling, the management of change.

As we have implied, our perception 20 years ago was probably wrong. Successful schools then knew about change but nobody chronicled it. Even that is not quite fair, since a glance at HMI's *Ten Good Schools* or Rutter's *Fifteen Thousand Hours* would confirm by implication, though not by express treatment, that such was what outstanding practitioners were doing. They didn't make it explicit.

What distinguished the outstanding department in school from another less successful department was the development – change by another name – they always seemed to have in train. So the primary teacher who spends the weekend spotting the materials that will be really useful in Monday's lesson, or the head of department restlessly considering the next stage in curriculum extension or laboratory improvement or resource-based learning or whatever are all practising the most worthwhile sort of curriculum change linked to change in the individual child or group of pupils. It is, of course, the hallmark of good teachers who know that change is their stock in trade – the outcome of sharp observation of each pupil and fitting their individual needs to the range of curricula and classroom techniques available.

What is new is the external agenda of change. The external availability of change has always been a useful tool to the leader who wants to initiate development:

> Well, it looks as though we will have to do it sooner or later so I thought we might as well make a start.
>
> (Headteacher comment to staff meeting)

In those far-off days, however, you could demonstrate change more readily because it was of an optional nature: there was more room for 'bottom-up' ownership. Many departments and schools in the hands of skilful leadership – usually where it was shared – were able to establish their own developments from their own critical confidence in their own practice. Internally generated change is the best sort of change, and we would justify the word 'best' because such change recharges energy in participants and embraces the greatest likelihood of improvement in teaching and learning styles, simply because it is so localised. It stands the most chance of generating magic moments in the classroom.

Nowadays, the hailstorm of externally mandated change is overwhelming and socially disturbing to the rhythms of successful teaching, learning and schooling. New methods of dealing with it are extensive. We have noticed in recent years the widespread introduction of development planning. It seems to us that the development plan has very little to do with what the experts say is its purpose, namely collective review of shared values. What it does provide, however, is the ability for a school to hold back the speed of externally mounted change.

As one headteacher said:

> The development plan provides the alibi and a useful tool with which to stage out the external agenda into manageable time slots

Time and time again our schools have shown an amusement about the implementation of the National Curriculum which is now wearing thin. Initial enthusiasm for curriculum change gave way to amusement with the first revisions, but with each successive variation order in the attainment targets, teacher enthusiasm is in real danger of being replaced by chronic cynicism. Perversely, the development plan, also provided by the government, affords a weapon to hold at arm's length the worst excesses of the result of the agenda of change.

It seems to us that in those schools that are best weathering the hailstorm of change there is a clearly understood range of stances. Everyone knows the private uncertainty any individual is experiencing. They know, too, that it differs among different members of the community. They also acknowledge that, for sanity's sake, there is a collective need to be reasonably positive in believing that, as one put it:

> Once the dust has settled we shall find that what we have always believed in is still true.

Nevertheless, there is also a recognition that in public, to parents, there is a need to put on a braver face still. The schools are unhappy about that:

> Who can afford to speak up? Certainly not me. In a competitive market it would appear we were failing.

Nevertheless, it has been interesting for us to observe that in some schools all these tensions are well understood by the governing body. Such schools have adopted yet another stance within the privacy of the staffroom, specifically turning the agenda to the internal rhythms of development, taking risks by using pressure either to rectify weaknesses amongst their staff team or to move them on. In the healthiest schools, this threefold emphasis – in private, in the staffroom and in public – is openly acknowledged in governors' meetings where all the stakeholders meet, confident that the reconciliation of these three approaches embraces the key to success. The touchstone of whether the key fits is usually found in implicit debates about the value systems of schools: the school tests any innovation against its implied or explicit values. For another school, the process is more systematic: it considers the change against its own value system, which is expressed in the aims, objectives and principles of the school. Some call it the ubiquitous 'mission statement'.

Having established that change is desirable, the leader often introduces it pretty quickly, not intending to allow too much opportunity for opposition. The presentation of three or four options about *how* to introduce the change rather than *whether* to do it at all is a time-honoured ploy for avoiding the uncomfortable danger of losing the change altogether by people voting it down! By that we mean the propensity for groups of people to defer to a noisy minority when they would be quite content to go along with the change in any case. So the adoption phase of change is best kept short.

The implementation phase is another matter.

The implementation phase

Time, interests and resources

Once change has been decided upon, there is an urgent need to be skilled in the process of its implementation. So many changes in schools have floundered because the initial interests of the originators and leaders were overtaken by other pressing priorities. Visible and continuing interest from the very top of the school and the department or key stage is therefore essential if change is to be implemented successfully. If individual and respected governors can show interest in the change that will help too.

Time therefore needs to be built into the headteacher's diary and those others mentioned to ensure that good intentions translate into reality. Time is also necessary to secure the ownership of those affected by change. So INSET days, meeting schedules and agendas have to be reviewed to ensure that there is extra time built in to review the first steps in the proposals for change so that they are approached in a way which offers some reasonable hope of them being successfully negotiated. Successful major changes, in our experience, have usually been accompanied by residential conferences or planning seminars for the key participants – crucially, both for those involved in the original design and then subsequently for those involved in the delivery. Encouraging the *team* approach means far less likelihood of the whole enterprise collapsing when a key player leaves.

> We all remember the time when we introduced the changed day because the group who planned it put on a skit at the staff party illustrating in bizarre fashion all the disasters we had anticipated the change would cause. The wine and the occasion made everyone helpless with laughter.
>
> (Member of staff recalling the initial opposition to a change in the timetable and the introduction of an activities week)

The need for a fixer

The person expected to lead innovation carries a great responsibility. If the wrong person is chosen, an extra hazard is created to the successful implementation of the innovation. We used to believe that many innovations failed simply because schools recruited people new to the school to lead the change, but now we are not so sure. Certainly, we have seen innovations fail in such circumstances but closer scrutiny suggests that it is the qualities and characteristics of the leaders and managers of the great change that matter. Essentially they need to be *'fixers'*. We do not mean that word in the pejorative 'president's men' sense, but we do see the need for the fixer to be someone who has a keen nose for potential trouble and, in particular, a built-in radar system to spot and neutralise the *'wreckers'*. This last group of people are those who have come on board only reluctantly and are waiting for the innovation to fail so that they can say 'I told you so.' So the fixer does need full knowledge of the views of other members of staff, either through their own experience or through briefing from an assistant. That explains our original, if false, conclusion that a newcomer was likely to fail. Clearly, well-briefed and supported, newcomers can succeed just as well as others with inside knowledge.

The implementation team

So many schools and other organisations get teams together prior to implementation but fail to see the need for a team to be responsible to be the critical friend and aide to the fixer who is asked to lead the implementation. Just as shared teamwork leads to agreement on new courses of action, so shared monitoring of the evidence of the implementation stage increases the chances of a shared sense of ownership of the enterprise. It is here that it is important to have the sceptic in the staffroom, unless they are an absolute wrecker, in the team rather than outside.

Features of progress: built-in review

Especially if a change is contentious, it is helpful to put a series of milestones into the plan for implementation, with success criteria attached to the milestones and an end-date for a review of the success of the scheme. 'If a thing is worth doing at all, it is worth doing badly' is an always startling, if well-known, aphorism that has its place in change management. Clearly, the planned change has got to be for the better but there needs to be a healthy recognition that the first time of doing anything is not going to be without blemish. Moreover, such an early acknowledgement of the limited efficacy of any change, at least initially, and the need to take stock subsequently, will ensure that the reluctant members of staff are more inclined to give the innovation the benefit of the doubt.

The consolidation phase

Once innovations have been adopted in principle, planned and implemented, they are adjusted after their initial phase, as they need to be institutionalised. So often we don't see the relationship of the changes we have implemented to the existing practices of the school. The latter may be in conflict with the former. The most obvious example that comes to mind is the continuation of blue and pink forms (for boys and girls respectively) after a school has decided to implement schemes to do with equal opportunity and gender on a much more far-reaching scale. There are many other examples. The attempt to get language across the curriculum accepted in the subject departments using the school library is hardly going to be helped if the librarian decides and orders the bookstock. The same library is not going to be complementary to a school's new-found determination to promote homework and supported self-study if it is locked and closed to pupils at break and lunchtimes and after school. Most of us live with institutional viruses analogous to computer viruses. If we leave them unattended the whole thrust of what we are trying to achieve will be frustrated. The fight against institutional viruses can be powerfully aided by the kind of standards maps referred to in chapter 4 (see Table 4.1–4.7), and which are being developed both across subject departments and for whole-school purposes within Birmingham.

Change, therefore, which Michael Fullan correctly called 'the journey of learning not a blueprint of certainty', is key to a school's continuing success. No headteacher, no head of department, indeed we think no teacher, can really reach the heights of what is possible without a more than passing competence in the management of change.

Some questions to consider in the management of change

Some prior considerations

- Does the proposed change fit with the school's or department's values?
- Will the change affect for the better teaching and learning? If so, how? How do those who achieve least success benefit from the proposed change? If not, why are we doing it?
- Does it fit/reinforce our priorities?
- How will it enable people to be more successful?
  Don't forget, some changes, especially timetable/curriculum changes, have an opportunity cost to other staff and pupils.
- Be clear about the phase of change. Which phase are we in? Is it *adoption, implementation* or *consolidation*?

- Is the change externally *required*, externally *available* or *internally generated*?
  Don't forget it is unwise ever to ignore internally generated proposals of change. The other two categories must be made to suit internal need.

Adoption

- Are we ensuring that all likely to be involved feel that they have made some input to the likely decision?
- Are we being careful to outline options for the method of effecting change rather than whether it is to be carried out?
- Are we alert to the *barnacles of change* – the ways in which old arguments and rivalries can be attached by participants to the innovation, thus slowing it up?
- Are we avoiding *false claims* for the proposed change's benefits?
  Don't forget, people will judge the change by standards higher than they applied to the previous state of affairs.
- If it is organisational change, does it have *curriculum* implications? If so, how are they to be facilitated?
- If it is curriculum or assessment change, does it have *management* implications? If so, how are they to be facilitated?
- Have we identified our *fixer* – the person who knows the system and is influential and commands respect among the staff and will therefore have a chance of bringing the change to fruition?
- Have we been careful to promise a *review* at all stages so that improvements and changes can be made?

Implementation

- Has the fixer identified or brought on side, key participants?
  Don't forget, some people may be happy not to be involved but nobody wants to be left out.
- Can someone's personal need (e.g. the professional development of the leader of the change) be allied to the collective need represented by the change?
  Don't forget, many changes that fail do so because either the wrong person is put in charge, or the right person is but they are overloaded.
- Have we allowed sufficient resources – especially time – for the implementation stage to work effectively?

- Is the leader of the school (or the agency outside the school which is identified with initiating the change if it is external) showing sufficient interest in the scheme?

  Don't forget, such people cannot show too much interest – and frequently the absence of interest is the cause of abortive implementation.

- Have we identified whether the change affects information, ideas, skills and attitudes? If the change affects skills, have we provided *coaching* to help people to learn the new ways of doing this? And are the coaches respected?

  Don't forget, many outside consultants/advisers/advisory teachers don't carry credibility with staff. Some do – and when they do they are invaluable change agents.

- Are *social events* arranged to help make the change enjoyable and in so doing, consolidate the direction of the change?

  Residentials, even for a few key staff, can be a powerful team-building exercise.

- Has the leader appointed to be responsible for the innovation the clout to do the job?

  Remember, this may have nothing to do with money or status, though they may matter. It is a lot to do with the perception of the leader by others. Their title may be important – but not as much as their ability to lead the school/department and the different personalities involved.

Consolidation

- Have we reviewed existing administrative functions to make sure they don't conflict with the direction intended for the innovation?
- How do we continue to show interest in the progress of the innovation?
- Have we established any features of progress or success criteria? How are they monitored? Who knows they are being monitored?
- How does the success feature in the school's rites and rituals?

The essential characteristics of leadership

We think we have seen in successful leadership, whether of schools or departments, the following features:

- A consistent set of *values* are the first necessity.
- Certain *qualities* are helpful – although by no means a universal set.

- *Competence* in a few *activities* (i.e. delegation, time management and the management of change) is crucial.

Where the values and competence have not been present the schools and departments seem to us to be on a downwards spiral.

> *Bring to mind for a moment the negative aspects of failing schools . . . empty libraries which are rarely visited . . . equipment and resources which are ill-treated . . . high rates of illiteracy in the pupils' home language . . . worsening exam performance . . . high absentee rates amongst pupils and staff . . . a depressing environment, visually, aurally and in the violent behaviour, orally and physically of one to another . . . these features require transformation.*

Our contention is simply that the unpleasant features we describe have established their grip on the institution through *failure* of leadership. Moreover, we would go so far as to say that the transformation of these features to success would not be accomplished without the application at various levels in the school of consistent values, a competence in the three key activities of delegation, time management and the management of change and even, in the worst-case scenario we have painted, the qualities we describe. Those qualities – cheerfulness, optimism, celebration of others – need to pervade the atmosphere. They are conducive to a catholic view and expectation of success. Some individuals – even leaders – can lack them, provided those individuals are known, despite the outward and visible evidence, to possess the inward and invisible certainty of quiet generosity.

So that turns us from values, qualities and competence to the *context* of leadership.

The context of leadership: three phases

The first phase of headship: initiation

> They hang on your every word and believe the idlest aside is a serious intention. I have concluded that it is best to behave like a Trappist – except they would read lots into the way you look. You have got to keep your own counsel in the early weeks – I am surprised how lonely it is. I am not sure they have been used to trust.
>
> (Headteacher, seven weeks into post)

Similarities between the classroom and the head's study are remarkable. Just as the teacher new to a school – even those with long years of successful experience in their first job – will often confess to 'feeling just like a probationer again', so it is for headteachers and heads of department who are new to the school in which they take up their post of responsibility.

In our research it was clear that there was a discernible difference in this phenomenon arising from whether the appointment was from within – as is increasingly the case, as governors have more say at the expense of LEAs in appointments. The comment of the headteacher seven weeks into the job is simply not echoed by the deputy promoted to be headteacher or, for that matter, the second in the department who succeeds their predecessor. They are known. They carry with them, however, another set of issues. It is, for example, very difficult for them to change their emphasis or perceived role. Their leadership style is well known, albeit from a different position of power. It has depended, successfully or not, on a set of perceived accommodations but it is now to be exercised in carrying out certain tasks which are quite different from those which they previously exercised. So the insiders in our research have great difficulty in achieving change. There are for them typically two scenarios. On the one hand, an insider will have been appointed because they seemed to be just the person to sustain the existing state of affairs – 'a safe pair of hands', 'better the devil you know than the one you don't' – with the likelihood, of which they are keenly aware, that the school or the department tails off as it clings on to the status quo and loses the vital ingredient of intellectual curiosity.

On the other hand, their appointment stems, more often than not, from the fact that they have only been in their previous post a short time, and are not implicated in the previous undesirable state of affairs. They have the confidence of governors – or senior management in the case of a department – and sometimes staff themselves – that they can lift the school (or the department) to new heights. They represent, even though they are from within, 'a fresh start'. The burden of expectation is enormous.

> They expect me to do so much so quickly. I have been there as deputy so they know what I would like to do and now the head has gone, they expect it all to happen overnight.
> (Female headteacher of Group 11 school, nine weeks into post)

Once again, context is all. For the 'outsider' assuming leadership, there is a small period of time when change can be effected. So much depends on the new leader's confidence and perception and there is the problem of knowing far less about a situation than will be the case after one has been there a year or so. Decisions could therefore be dramatically wrong. But the school is expecting, even wanting, change. Nevertheless, staff want to be honoured and respected. They don't want the newcomer to fall into the trap of referring to 'when they were in such and such a school', whenever they are commending some new practice, effortlessly conveying, in the process, a feeling of exclusion and incompetence to staff both in the reference to the other place and in their use of the first-person singular or plural. More subtly, heads frequently make the mistake of always measuring the school's progress from the moment they themselves arrived there. So two years in, sentences start 'in the last two years . . .', and eight years in 'in the last eight years . . . we have achieved' this, that or the other. Of course, the longer the head has been at the school, the less that matters since the likelihood is that the staff have themselves arrived since the date in question!

The really successful leader finds something of value to honour in the legacy they have inherited. They try to avoid the pitfall represented by the following:

> I knew the school was underachieving: I was invited to present my vision to the staff. It was professional development day and it was my first at the school. I socked it to them straight. I said I knew the children were under-performing and that collectively they had no self-respect. And I was going to help them change all that.
> (Headteacher who stayed three turbulent years in an 11–18 school)

So the first few days, weeks, months and year represent the first stage of headship. The staff are looking for actions to match the words of the newcomer. Most importantly, the words are heard at staff assemblies and staff meetings.

> We never really knew Mr Walton. He was very good at the external meetings and the PR. He was a big man but I never really quite trusted him: at school assemblies you never knew what he stood for. So he gave the school a good local image but there was no substance behind it – we were the same old school we had been in Miss Horrocks's time and we hadn't really changed one jot. Mr Walton stayed five years and of course he came unstuck during the teachers' action. He made promises – well, not exactly promises but he had given you to understand, you know, and just left you with the impression that an allowance would follow if you did what he hoped. So when the unions wanted us to take action we did – not that we liked doing it for the kids but we wanted to get rid of him. We simply felt let down. Now Mr Hall (the new head) is a different kettle of fish altogether. He is still good with the locals – the heads of the primary schools really trust him. But in the first assembly he ever took, you could see that he meant business, said what he'd expect of everybody and proved he meant it. We have changed a lot in the year and a half he has been here. Really, we have all tried. It is a much happier place and you see it in the behaviour of not just the children but the staff too. The results will soon follow I am sure'.
> (Long-standing allowance holder in 11–16 school)

Staff meetings are fraught with difficulty, although less so for the confident newcomer than can be the case later in the head's stay at the school. In the first staff meeting, now more likely than not (and hazardously), on a professional development day, the head is invited to show their philosophy. They know that whatever they show in their words will be judged by their future actions.

The doubtful benefits of previous experience

If the head or head of department has held a similar post before, they bring with them the advantages of experience. Along with that sometimes comes the disadvantage of forgetting how long it takes to get the trust of staff. It is also a handicap some of those new to the experience sometimes fail to realise. There is no doubt, however, that to follow one successful leadership position with another can play tricks with the memory about how long it takes to make progress.

> You forget what it means to be unknown. You take short cuts which you could get away with in the last place. It won't work here though and [through forgetting that] I have probably set myself back a long way.
>
> (Female head commencing second headship)

In the first few days of headship, there are problems to face up to. Nowadays some are different in kind from those of the past, while others have a perennial feel about them which will be recognised by successive generations of new headteachers or heads of departments. In the wake of Local Management of Schools (LMS), however, the likelihood of inheriting a massive deficit is greater than it used to be when the LEA controlled all finance save capitation. It was always possible in those days for the LEA to make up the deficit to the school on capitation from the much greater central reserve. Even if there were the will to do it now, there is no longer the way.

It is quite frequently the case, therefore, that new heads are having to make one, two, three, even seven or eight staff redundant in the first term. Experienced heads also know the often contrived but watertight ways in which selections for such redundancies are made on the basis of 'curriculum need': it is a particularly difficult judgement to get right in one's first term. The silver lining to this particular cloud is that nobody blames the newcomer for so traumatic an experience. They almost always know that it is the previous head's fault.

The second stage of headship: the development stage

During the second stage of headship people are frequently characterised as being engaged in implementing an extending agenda of improvements. Leaders who were deputies in the same context are often into the second stage of leadership before they know it.

Those who are new heads will start the second phase at the point at which staff in particular and the wider community too, know that their early words and actions have that unfailing consistency of a bell that is pealing with a true

ring. It is as though there is no longer even the remotest suspicion that subsequent actions will be inconsistent.

> Oh, we know it must be OK. It may look odd but with Yvonne she
> will always have a reason. She knows more than we do.
> (On a pupil being sent to the head and receiving a sanction
> different from that which the staff expected)

For successful heads in this second stage, however, there is an increasing willingness to be participants because they have relaxed and they know they can
rely on staff to sustain the direction of the school. This is particularly so if a
school has been turned round into a confident new direction: people grow and
developments multiply and there is no wish to return to the old days.

> She has the knack of getting the best out of you. Take John [head of
> science] – he seems to have taken on a new lease of life since Yvonne
> came. He reviewed all the science programmes and started a science
> club, and he is not the only one.

The leader has the supportive thanks of the staff because order has been established and a new sense of direction confirmed. The rest of the school and
community can now contribute in increasing measure to the school's accom-
plishments.

Leaders in the second phase therefore need to change their style – at least in
the sense that they spend their time on different tasks. The initiatives that they
have set in motion continue to need their attention, as do all the groups who
have a claim on the leader's time and attention. But, as we have already
implied, the successful leader can be more discerning about how much time is
given to each and in what rhythm. What originally needed daily attention can
now be undertaken from time to time, since confidence and autonomy have
grown and become self-generating.

When a leader is making a real success of the second phase, they sometimes
ask whether a direction that they personally initiated is, after all, the right one.
It is a mark of relaxed confidence.

> I know we pushed it then as a priority – the shift in the
> timetabling of PSE – but maybe I got it a bit wrong. Not everyone
> is giving it their best shots – not because they didn't want to or
> because they don't think it is important – but it is simply not on
> top of their own personal agenda of priorities and they don't feel
> comfortable with it.
> (Head instituting review of personal and social education
> programme which he had majored on when
> he had arrived three years earlier)

It is very important for the leader who makes the transition from the initiation phase into the development stage to have a rough idea how they will know that the development phase itself is exhausted. Of course, life may be so full of mutual reward that the phase lasts a dozen or more years – a kind of never-ending, internally generated energy supply. The likelihood of it lasting depends on constant renewal, so visits to other places to meet other people doing the same job can help. That is why the best heads of department are active in the subject and in other professional associations. It is why mutual visiting helps the intellectual curiosity of the teacher/leader to be sustained.

> I always do a day at Abbey Science Department and Ann comes to us once a year too. Part of our agenda is to share what we have learnt from all the new blood we each get into our department. I wish we could do more of it. We meet socially too – the families get on providing we promise not to talk too much shop for too much of the time.
>
> (Head of science)

The same is true of our successful headteachers. In that respect the development of peer group visits in headteacher appraisal seems a promising development for extending the creativity of the second phase of headship. So too, the encouragement of benchmarking.

It is three or four years into this stage that big decisions not grasped in the first phase can be tackled. Credit will be strong enough after about that time for the odd deferred unpopular decision to be gripped. Almost always it will be to do with personnel. Time and time again the descriptions of a running sore in a staffroom, which must be tackled if it is not to become a fatal wound, crop up in our conversations about schools. It nearly always refers to the member of staff whom everybody humours but all secretly dislike, who sometimes lies low when a newcomer appears, instinctively sucking up to the new leader to the disgust of the rest of the department or the school before showing their true – and false – colours. The larger the organisation, the more likely it is that such a person (or people) will find places to survive on a change of leadership. The real test of leadership, however, comes in showing that such issues will be grasped rather than endlessly avoided. Indeed, it is not too much to say that if the leader avoids the issue for too long, they hasten the advent of the third phase, the phase of decline and withdrawal.

Before turning to the third phase of leadership we think it worth identifying a further subtlety about the second phase. It does not appear to us that the second phase is smooth. By that we mean that it appears to be capable of being lengthened by successive waves of renewal.

> We thought we were a school that was getting somewhere. We weren't yet 'cosy' but I thought we were in danger of becoming so. I

mean, 'comfortable' is a word that is appropriate for school life, but not 'cosy' . . . somehow or other I thought we needed renewal . . . so did John [the head] . . . the opportunity came when John took half a term out on visits . . . He came back and called the staff together . . . That's when we did the strengths, weaknesses, opportunities, threats [SWOT] analysis . . . let me see, it was three years ago. John had been with us seven years then. It is from that date we got our second wind.

(Deputy head of 11–16 school)

Certainly, in some of our schools heads and staff identified the need for periodic new directions. In one they thought they had cracked it through a systematic collective review of all practices in their staff handbook. While it seemed to us that such a systematic approach was a powerful help, and certainly an antidote to complacency or cosiness, it didn't quite capture what we had in mind. We are trying to convey the impression of the need from time to time for leaders to be invigorated and to take on new directions – even adopt a new style – within a school. Signposts plus symbolic action are what may signal such a change.

What was clear was that in the successful schools we encountered, the initiation phase of leadership soon became developmental and that the third phase – that of decline – could be held off by second, third and even fourth waves of new energy and direction, spaced out at roughly five-yearly intervals within what we have called the developmental phase. The rhythms of these waves are becoming dangerously choppy as a result of implementation of government-imposed external change, which cannot be sensitive to the internal chemistry of a school.

The case of the failing head of department

Milvenham School sits in its own grounds on a leafy edge of a rural West Midlands town. Its children attend from 11 until 16. John Narbett has been head for five years. Everyone liked him at first; he was a 'breath of fresh air', open, energetic and committed to a positive approach to all his staff and school community. He knew that to be welcoming and cheerful was to spread warmth. The school generally, in the words of the local community, 'tightened up its act'. It profited by the happy conjunction of his appointment and the end of the teachers' dispute with the government, which had been devastating so far as staff morale was concerned, not least because it bruised the shared value system, hard won over a decade or more since the school had opened as a comprehensive. The founding head had left with an obvious mixture of emotions.

The head of science, Roland Barnes, is the school representative for one of the teachers' unions and had enjoyed considerable 'disruptive power' during the time of the teachers' disputes. Roland was 43 and disappointed: he had founded the science department and been passed over just before John's arrival for the deputy headship. He had tasted power during the time of the teachers' dispute and this reinforced his view that if it hadn't been for Helen his wife, he would have moved on to a deputyship elsewhere five years earlier. Now he knew he couldn't find the energy to run the science department any more. 'My heart is no longer in teaching,' is how he put it to us. 'It fills up the hours but I would like to run an outdoor education centre. I have bought a farmhouse in mid-Wales and Helen and I are doing it up at the weekends and in the holidays. Give me another six and a half years and I can take early retirement and go. In the meantime I am taking out what I have put in.'

During our time with the school, John Narbett had discovered, too late in his first year, that such was Roland's real agenda. Roland had simply kept quiet about everything. Now, as we could see, he used every working party, every steering group and every meeting, to puncture the atmosphere. Presumably he merely hoped to pave the way for a thankful early retirement as he approached his fiftieth birthday. John Narbett, however, was not going to wait: he had been in the school three years and at the end of our fieldwork had spent some time fretting about the issue, knowing that Barnes was always just the right side of acceptable behaviour. Moreover, the annual analysis of exam results, which Narbett had instituted on his arrival, was revealing a fatal weakness right at the heart of the curriculum. Individual pupils' performance in science simply didn't measure up to what they had achieved in maths, English and modern languages. The reaction of Roland Barnes was clever. He actually concealed his own bad teaching by swapping teachers midway though Year 11, supposedly in order 'to bring another teacher's skills to bear on improving results in GCSE' but in reality to conceal his own incompetence behind what John Narbett called 'a snowstorm of anti-radar activity'.

John Narbett levelled with Roland Barnes. Lessons starting late, books unmarked, no out-of-school commitment to revision classes, bad results. The science adviser was brought in and within three terms Barnes had resigned at the age of 48 to take his chance in Wales.

In the three terms that it took me to achieve his resignation after four years of sniping, I actually knew I had no friends among the staff who thought I was being unnecessarily tough. But it had to be done.

It was evident two terms later that Narbett had judged the issue correctly. The staff who spoke to us were openly relieved that a troublemaker had gone. The science staff had a new lease of energy and the school's science results had already shown significant improvement.

The third phase of headship: decline and withdrawal

There are some leaders who never make their mark, whose second phase is in reality the third phase of headship – the painful decline and withdrawal.

Almost all leaders, however good, have a brief evening when they lose their power and cease to plan for improving tomorrow because they know that that day will bring another set of challenges in another job or in the next stage of their personal and professional lives. For some it may be just before retirement itself. It is precisely because they have lost their vision of the future that they cease to be leaders.

That won't be my job – I'll leave the issue to my successor to decide.

It is something that everybody who has moved from one job to another will recognise. Clearly, the shorter that period can be the better.

The problem in senior leadership positions, for example in headship, is that one can imagine entering the decline and withdrawal phase because of the overwhelming quantity of the external agenda. Moreover, to this are added the increased social problems of children and their families, so that the familiar feeling of schools is frequently the resolution of a series of crises. Leaders know, however, when they lose that ability to hover above events with half their mind so that they can see the individual actions within the context of the wood. Indeed, if the real human problems so dominate the leader that they displace the longer view, the whole school or department is in trouble.

> I noticed I was busy: it was essentially displacement activity. I was busy simply putting off the big tasks, the tackling of the problems because I couldn't see the solutions any longer. I knew in the end that I never would: it was time to go, to give way to someone else who could do it. I stayed three years too long.
>
> (Retired head of 11–16 school talking of the last three years of leadership)

Some people shift dangerously beyond the freedom of the post, to exploit its licence. Some of us, reflecting on this, have coined the phrase describing the mercifully brief third phase as the 'decline into the bunker phase'. We meant to encompass by that a double allusion. For some heads it becomes a phase of unrealistically hanging on stubbornly to ways of doing things long after they have ceased to be appropriate to present needs; for others the displacement activity consists of more frequent visits to the golf course or such places where formerly life had been kept in balance by recreation, but which are now an escape, blotting out a reality in which events are in control of the leader rather than vice versa. Sadly, many leaders stay just a bit too long for their own and their school's good.

> If you are really thinking of doing something else, don't tell anyone until the last minute. it is not fair to the school to know their head has really got his/her mind on something else. They depend on her/him to guard the vision. They can't be doing with someone wondering all the time about their own future.
>
> (Same headteacher of 11–16 school
> reflecting on their retirement)

The optimum leadership style

With all sorts of doubts and hesitations, we nevertheless do feel from our studies that we can identify an optimum style of leadership. We do not preclude people of all sorts operating in our preferred style: it is not confined to extroverts or introverts, charismatic or retiring figures exclusively, but incorporates both.

The perceptive professional developer: the problem solver and the motivational leader

Earlier we noted some leaders' capacity to sweep away problems, not by minimising them, still less by ignoring them, but mainly by turning them into opportunities for growth and development. Moreover, if they hadn't this gift themselves, they recognised its need and were good at identifying people in the organisation who had it to a sufficiently greater or lesser extent. In short, if such leaders are not instinctively blessed themselves with the capacity, they recognise the need for such people and promote them to a place in the sun, both within their management team and, if they are perceptive about people, more widely within individual departments and in whole-school working parties and extra-curricular activities such as trips, drama, music and sport. Moreover, these leaders move beyond 'order' and 'relationships' in their activities and find ways of engaging the staff in continually exhilarating discussions about the purposes of the school. It is as though the school has a magic carpet of burgeoning ideas, some of which are impossible dreams but all of which convey an excitement, a sense of mission which sustains them in the troughs, cushioning the bumps of daily crises. In short, we see three levels of activity in leadership, as represented below:

Level 1   Order
Level 2   Order + relationships
Level 3   Order + relationships + curriculum/professional development

Rather like the National Curriculum assessment arrangements, we think there is a hierarchy of performance in leadership, whether it applies to the classroom, in the department or at the school level. We have represented it as shown. Once you are a level 3 leader, you need to move occasionally from one to the other aspect in order to keep each in good health. The teacher who concentrates so hard on the curriculum that they ignore the basics of order will find it very difficult to sustain learning. The lessons may be great in theory, immaculate, as it were, in conception, but because the teacher hasn't mastered the basics of classroom organisation and management or is ignoring them, the pupils can't take advantage of them. One can think of many a beginning teacher who encounters such teaching difficulties: it probably lies at the root of the perennial advice 'don't smile until Christmas' which veterans give young entrants.

In the same way, once people are comfortable with each other – when they know who they are, as it were – it is possible to establish a pleasant working relationship. So leaders of this sort are very good at established frameworks of praise rather than of criticism or punishment. Social occasions abound: birthdays are remembered, small thoughtful gestures surprise everybody. North pole–north pole leaders whom we described earlier have insurmountable difficulties in trying to establish the willingness, the generosity, the sheer goodwill which getting level 2 leadership right demands. So any attempt they make at level 3 is always hobbled by a failure at the heart of the activity.

The third level is elusive in any case. It is like a slippery bar of soap. How do we establish a self-critical evaluative climate? Leaders determined to develop their level of leadership deploy forms of collective review or self-evaluation in order to spread the intellectual curiosity about teaching, learning and the curriculum beyond the individual classroom. They may use GRIDS analysis or a variety of other measures to get started but once they have it established they give it a spin from time to time to keep the quality alive. Certainly, those headteachers who don't keep themselves abreast of the developments in each subject area will have difficulty in sustaining level 3 leadership across the board.

It is in the third level of leadership that headteachers' actions and how they use their time become critically important. Increasingly, we see two sorts of leaders among the perceptive professional developers in the schools we visit: the problem solvers and the motivational leaders.

The charismatic leader

This leader has qualities that attract others. They are north pole–south pole and aware of its dangers. They tend towards flamboyance; they are sometimes impulsive and often assertive – all the characteristics of front-of-house leadership come to mind. They will be first over the top in any crisis. They will be cheerful and optimistic. All the qualities which make these people natural leaders are an ever-present warning to make sure that others have a place in the sun. Their vision can blind and their strong personality cast a shadow over the need for shared leadership. All their strengths need to be critically monitored and kept in rein in order to enable others to develop their contribution to the school's development. The danger for these leaders is that development becomes entirely dependent on them and the school becomes the co-ordination of the ad hoc, especially in the third phase of decline. They fall into the habit of telling more frequently than they listen because they become rooted in their own perception of values rather than the subtleties provided by others. In the end – that is in the leader's declining phase – people stay quiet because they know they will not be valued.

The back-room leader

Some people are *organisation leaders*. Their strength lies in enabling systems to work well. They understand the need for systems to work effectively and efficiently. They have policies and agreed practices for all eventualities. Job descriptions are clear, minutes appear on time, things work like clockwork. The danger of these leaders is that they overlook the need for 'flair', 'the out of the ordinary', the 'taking of risks'. They may become too clinical. In the third, declining, phase, the organisation leader often becomes passive or political, sitting on the fence and failing to take a lead when it is needed. They still see every point of view but now they fail to adopt any one at all when the school clearly needs it. Sometimes these leaders are too quick to criticise, too fond of blaming others. In the end they become puzzled when the system doesn't work any more.

In our studies we became convinced that both types of leader can succeed. Instead of regretting into which broad category they instinctively fall, the leaders 'who know who they are' will be wise to ride with the strength of their style and work to bring out the complementary talents of those many people who share their leadership. We hope too that by reading this they will be able to move from initiation to implementation and have a greater skill in skimming the top of successive waves of development in a creative and long-lasting second stage. We hope too that they will recognise the onset of the damaging third phase and surprise and disappoint everyone by leaving.

Above all, we have become convinced that vision is the outcome of many people's contributions, certainly not something which originates with one person. Even where the charismatic leader gives voice to the vision, its legitimacy lies in the fact that it is a shared product. The leader's essential duty in respect of vision is to recognise it and act as its guardian, ensuring that someone, not necessarily them, gives it an outing from time to time.

Some questions leaders need to ask

Leadership in others

- Who are the leaders in our school among teachers, parents, pupils and governors?
- Who are the leaders in our various departments and what opportunities have they for leadership?
- At what stage are people at in their leadership of particular activities first, second or third?
- Which members of staff are people who instinctively resist failure and bad news and whose emphasis is preoccupied by the positive and by success? How do we spread their influence?
- When people in our school/department are given opportunities for leadership, are the circumstances conducive to a successful outcome? Have they support and resources? Are the persons identified with responsibilities well suited to the task in hand, that is the cycles of planning, organising, providing, maintaining, monitoring and evaluating?
- How do we guard against the leaders in our school disabling others by the strength of their vision?
- How are those who are leading doing so by their actions and their commitment in practice?

Time

- How does my use of time (last week/last term) reflect the importance I attach to various parts of school life?
- How do I keep abreast of the latest curriculum developments in all the subjects, not merely the ones I like? Do the staff in these areas know I am interested? If so, how?
- What time do I give to the out-of-school timetable?
- How far do I engage in 'displacement activity' to avoid difficult issues?
- When did I last speak to – and listen to -
    a junior member of staff?
    a member of the support staff?
    a member of the governing body?
    the neighbours/householders/shopkeepers near the school?
- What is my contribution towards making a new member of the community (staff or pupil) feel welcome and valued?

Behaviour towards others

- How do I express my *genuinely felt* gratitude to others for what they do for members of the school community?
- Have I let it be known, in private and firmly, when I see evidence that any member of the community is not trying their best? Do I try to find out why?
- When did I last 'take the blame' for a failing of another member of the community who had tried their hardest but brought us into risk?
- How welcoming am I to people in the corridor, in my office and in the street?
- What themes are used in assemblies and other public occasions to reinforce a programme of shared values about the sort of community the school wishes to become?

In their own words: shared values

It is so good to come here. The head has always got a cheerful 'good morning' for you. It is infectious . . . you become cheerful with your tutor group. She is careful to start four days of the week with a briefing – there is always a joke of some sort – well at least a lightness of touch . . . it is hard to explain. It is very special.

(Second year teacher of humanities, 11–16 school)

We start the day with a departmental breakfast – it is on Tuesdays, not every day. You can arrive really early on that day and John (the head of department) will be joking about the toast and what is to go on it – he brings something new each week. We all muck in – glad to – work's fun here.

(Science allowance holder, same school)

We end the week with the head – all the departmental heads that is. It is not really a meeting, more a drink before the weekend. You don't have to go but we all do, more times than not. Well, you don't want to miss it because that is where all the ideas, the dreams and the realities come together. I can think of lots of plans that were hatched there . . . and lots of wild ideas that never took off.

(Head of PE, same school)

'None of us really liked what he had started . . . it was a change we all said wouldn't work. But he had said 'Try it . . . we can always change back if it doesn't work'. He always does that when we are starting something new . . . says you can never get things absolutely right first time – mind you, he also says no reason not to try to get it as right as possible. Well, anyway, this time he knew – could sense it.

(Senior teacher, same school)

It takes a whole staff to make a successful school

In three schools recently there seemed to be a common theme – the growing importance of support staff. 'We were really surprised and very dismayed,' declared the primary head teacher. 'We all thought the school was good. All the things we as teachers valued seemed to us to indicate we were on the right lines. 'You've noticed', she went on, 'standards of display and you've commented on it. It *is* good. It has all the usual features when it is good: it reinforces language, maths. and you have noticed the puzzles to encourage thinking. The children look to the walls to enter competitions and trails. All the children have been celebrated. Our parents notice and like it.'

She paused with a look of remembered resignation. 'But when we surveyed our support staff – the classroom assistants, the integration workers, the midday supervisors – they hadn't a good word to say about either the display or any other aspect of school life for that matter.'

In the second school, the head was telling me about the influence of the secretary. 'Well, it's the same anywhere,' she confided. 'The secretary is the key to the whole school. She receives all the confidences of the school community – the staff, the pupils and the parents.' I immediately agreed, reflecting that I had already seen one secretary ruin a school because she would meddle by relaying messages she should have kept to herself. In the school where I was talking to the headteacher, the secretary was the hub of its success. She interpreted moods, received confidences, radiated warmth, humour and a sheer love of living which was contagious. The children saw her as the person to whom they gave news each morning and whose good opinion they sought. Discretion was her second name; wisdom her first.

At a third school – also a primary school, on an outer-ring estate – I was introduced to 'number three'. I never quite discovered why she was called 'number three'. She has been there for twelve years or so. They still pay her as a classroom assistant. She's more than that – she's simply a remarkable human being. She plays the piano, she creates the costumes for the school play; she organises and takes part in the annual school trip. It's her job (because she would have it no other way) to organise displays throughout the school and, as the head confides, 'I always put her with our newly qualified teachers. She is such a good role model.'

That set me thinking, as had the experience in the first school where the support staff were not involved, as the head's survey had shown. The head soon put matters to rights. A survey had shown not merely their poor view of a place where they worked but also that below the surface, they didn't feel valued. So-called 'non-teaching' staff had, unsurprisingly, felt they were 'non-persons'. The head explained how she had devised a new strategy which had begun to work and she backed her words with appropriate action. Money available through LMS was devoted to staff development for all staff, not simply teachers: the inclusion of support staff was now a matter of course on curriculum and other committees. There was parity of esteem in staff meetings and membership of the staffroom committee. Attendance was automatic at in-service days and there were opportunities to take part in all school activities, including the selection of all new staff. All this had occurred within the last three years.

It illustrates how approaches to staff development have moved on in our more participative and less hierarchical age. It's a good job things have moved on because the number of support staff in schools has risen, and so it should. In so many successful primary classrooms now there are two paid adults – a teacher and a support worker, variously called a classroom assistant, learning resources assistant, sometimes teacher assistant. In a few classrooms there are paid workers in support of integration for children with special educational needs.

3

TEACHING AND LEARNING

Learning can unlock the treasure that lies within us all. In the 21st century, knowledge and skills will be the key to success . . . Good teachers, using the most effective methods, are the key to higher standards.

(DfEE, *Excellence in Schools*, 1997)

The important thing is not so much that every child should be taught, as that every child should be given the wish to learn.

(John Lubbock)

The quality of teaching and learning is at the heart of school improvement and real, lasting change can only come from what teachers and learning assistants do consistently in classrooms and other learning areas in the school. Curiously, although schools have policies for almost everything, partly with an eye on the OFSTED inspection process, many schools still do not have policies on teaching and learning and it is sometimes difficult to ascertain from their practices whether these are based on an individual or a collective approach. In successful schools the staff have thought through together what constitutes effective teaching and learning in their particular context, based on a set of core values and beliefs, and they continue to speculate how they might improve their practice, involving pupils, parents and governors in the debate. They are aware that their central purpose and the focus of all their endeavours is raising the achievement of pupils and they engage in collaborative activity to ensure this. Principles are turned into processes and practices and once agreed strategies have been implemented they are constantly monitored, reviewed and adjusted again in the light of the evidence. Through this process there is an internal dynamic to teaching and learning and the school is geared to continuous improvement. There are high expectations for everybody, as both learners and teachers, and the headteacher in particular is a leader of learning. There is in fact an apparent teaching and learning culture in the school which is constantly being nourished and developed, with staff taking individual and collective responsibility to improve on their previous best, with reference to the best knowledge and practice available, and committing themselves to regular self-evaluation.

Educational change depends on what teachers do and think – it's as simple and as complex as that.

(Michael Fullan, *The New Meaning of Educational Change*, 1991, p. 117)

In considering how to improve a school through the development of a dynamic teaching and learning culture it may be best to start from the point of view of the new teacher who, full of hope and expectation – and certainly a little trepidation – joins the staff of a school on a permanent basis. All headteachers and teachers could usefully ask themselves how, simply by joining them, a new teacher would become a better teacher and would strengthen even more the critical mass of effective teaching. The new teacher, whatever their experience, may encounter various energy states within the school. To produce the right amount of energy to transform pupil achievement the school needs to have a high proportion of *energy creators* who:

- are enthusiastic and always positive
- use critical thinking, creativity and imagination
- stimulate and spark others
- practise leadership at all levels
- are able and willing to scrutinise their practice and willing to make their practice accessible to others
- wish to improve on their previous best

Above all, energy creators are rich with ideas and creativity and through their unfailing cheerfulness and optimism affect for the better the behaviour of the many *energy neutral* staff who are:

- competent, sound practitioners
- willing to service the task
- good at 'maintenance'
- sometimes uncomfortable accepting examination of their practice by others
- capable of improving on their previous best

Sadly, there may also be some *energy consumers* for whom every silver lining has many clouds and every glass is half empty. Such staff tend to:

- have a negative view of the world
- resent change and practise blocking strategies
- use other people's time excessively
- not feel good about themselves
- be unable and unwilling to critically examine their teaching practice
- appear not to want to improve on their previous best

These are the things which trigger energy, excitement, enthusiasm, effort, effervescence and enterprise. Everyone is full of 'e' in all its forms. The trick is to release that 'e' – the excitement as well as the effort, the enthusiasm as well as the energy. The more organisations can match these personal 'e' factors and bubble with them the more successful and fun they will be.

(Charles Handy, *Inside Organisations*, 1990, pp. 32–3)

We have referred previously to teachers as leaders and the task of schools is to develop their teaching culture so that everybody is an energy creator for at least part of the time and never less than neutral at other times. The new teacher is therefore energised immediately by simply joining the staff and is caught up in the excitement of teaching and learning. What would be the characteristics of such a teaching and learning culture and how may a school develop this? This chapter discusses the following ten features of such a culture which, if adopted, would help to improve all schools:

1 an agreed policy about the practice of teaching and learning
2 a teaching and learning staffroom
3 collaborative teaching, planning and assessment
4 the effective use of learning resources
5 monitoring and evaluation/collective review
6 professional development
7 action research
8 community involvement in the learning school
9 curriculum enrichment and extension
10 the celebration of teaching and learning

An agreed policy about the practice of teaching and learning

Such a policy would start from the basic question of whether the whole staff, which includes learning assistants and all those who contribute to the teaching and learning process, have discussed their ideas and beliefs about teaching and learning, and how best to raise standards of achievement. The policy would want to emphasise a shared philosophy and a shared language. It would cover the central issues of teaching and learning styles, teaching skills, the importance of questioning, resources for learning, and teaching and learning as the central concern of continuing professional development and support, as well as self evaluation and review. There is a vast amount of research literature on all these topics, but because context is so important it is essential that every member of staff, involving pupils, parents and governors as far as possible, hammers out their values, practices and expectations and make sure that this overall policy is translated into pedagogy at all levels within the school. Subject leaders, whether in primary, special or secondary schools, should be able to transmit the central messages effectively into their areas of the curriculum and work with groups of teachers on developing appropriate schemes of work and lesson plans. Teachers working in year groups or key stages should be able to base their planning on these overt principles, processes and practices and to monitor and evaluate accordingly. From all this will emerge a unity of purpose which is a condition of achieving consistency of educational practice across all staff in the school. A policy for teaching and learning could be constructed under the following headings:

- values, beliefs and principles
  the development of a shared language about the craft of teaching and the complexities of learning
- repertoire and range of teaching techniques, skills and strategies
  exposition and explanation, practical activities and investigations, the use of questions, discussion and problem solving; individual, group and whole-class teaching
- learning styles
  awareness of multiple intelligences, the need for differentiation, independent learning and critical thinking
- the use of learning resources
  a range of resources appropriate to pupils' age and needs, provision of information technology, reference materials, the role of the library/resource centre in supporting learning
- the effectiveness of planning
  continuity and progression of learning, the organisation of short-, medium- and long-term planning
- the use of assessment
  formative and summative assessment, the marking of work, the use of assessment information to inform curriculum planning
- high expectations and appropriate challenge
  appropriate tasks and teaching techniques for pupils of different abilities, accelerated learning, setting and banding
- creating and maintaining stimulating learning environments
  effective classroom organisation, interactive and whole-school displays, a climate of innovation
- monitoring and evaluating teaching and learning
  the collection of evidence and the critical reflection on policies and practices, action research

A school with clearly thought through and expressed policies and practices on teaching and learning would be able to state these in its recruitment literature and attract like-minded staff with an opportunity to reinforce these beliefs within the induction programme. Perhaps most tellingly of all, a school could institute the practice of making sure that all applicants were observed teaching as part of their recruitment strategy. This strategy reinforces the message of the critical importance of quality teaching in the school, but also has the benefit of involving pupils and other staff in the process of classroom observation and teacher selection. Already the new member of staff would feel part of an effective teaching culture simply by joining the staff and being ready to undertake a continuous programme of professional development securely anchored within a teaching and learning policy.

> Good teaching is not just a matter of being efficient, developing competence, mastering technique and possessing the right kind of knowledge. Good teaching also involves emotional work. It is infused with desire, pleasure, mission, creativity, challenge and joy. Good teaching is a profoundly emotional activity.
>
> (Andy Hargreaves, *Changing Teachers, Changing Times*, 1995)

A teaching and learning staffroom

It is essential to develop a teaching culture where talking frankly and knowledgeably about teaching is acceptable and enlightening. Most of this will be done informally in the staffroom. By talking about teaching, teaching staff develop further a shared language about the complexity of teaching and learning and constantly refine and sharpen their practice. Whilst we recognise the social nature of teaching and the necessity to relax in a staffroom, the room itself carries powerful messages about what should be the prime purpose of any school. Our new teacher may notice immediately that there is a staffroom noticeboard dedicated to the practice of teaching and learning and that there is an expectation that everybody takes it in turns, either individually or as a department, to provide appropriate materials such as newspaper articles, book reviews and generic teaching materials. Further, there is a staffroom library where teachers can gain easy access to key texts and information to help them speculate further on their practice. The teaching and learning policy of the school is displayed on the wall along with the targets outlined in the school development plan or OFSTED action plan. Perhaps there will be a computer dedicated to accessing ideas on teaching and learning either through the LEA or through national school improvement databases which act as a powerful network for teachers wanting to develop their practice and pedagogy.

Every one of us is both a learner and a teacher.

Some teaching staff are engaged on courses of study leading to further accreditation. They are known to everybody and everybody is asked to furnish examples of their practice or evidence from their classrooms relevant to their colleagues' research. The staff are used to contributing ideas about teaching and learning and here in the staffroom is a copy of their 'butterfly' book where they have all written down three practices which have had a disproportionate effect on the success of their teaching and learning strategies. They expect to contribute to an annual publication based on their action research, possibly around particular themes such as the teaching of reading, using information technology or classroom organisation. Also available in the staffroom is a collection of reports that teachers have written after returning from INSET days and courses out of school. These reports are written in such a format as to easily inform everyone's practice, and of course the author is available to go into more detail on request.

The staffroom is a place to learn with plenty of social and professional interaction and any new teacher or visitor, as well as the regular staff, feels stimulated, energised and informed by being there.

Good teachers create the environments that makes good teaching pay off.

Collaborative teaching, planning and assessment

The successful school will have a commitment to sharing and designing planning for learning and the preparation and dissemination of teaching and learning materials. The more that teachers work together in appropriate teams the more that a shared understanding emerges about the complexity of teaching and learning, with the aim of consistent improvement and the raising of pupil achievement. Normally this goes on in year or phase groups in primary schools and in departments in secondary schools, but sometimes it is episodic and not sufficiently thought through in terms of teaching strategies, learner responses and assessment. The repertoire and range of teaching strategies and the balance of whole-class teaching, group and individual work is a critical part of such planning and a process whereby teachers can teach each other the practice of teaching. The new National Literacy Strategy offers a succinct guide to successful teaching as being:

- discursive: characterised by high quality oral work
- interactive: pupils' contributions are encouraged, expected, and extended
- well-paced: there is a sense of urgency, driven by the need to make progress and succeed
- confident: teachers have a clear understanding of the objectives
- ambitious: there is optimism about and high expectations of success

---

The Year 6 class ignored me. The best classes often do. Well when you are busy there is no time for distractions. And this particular group were surrounded by novels, poems – their own and those of other great authors – and a fascinating vocabulary collection of 'words'. They had clearly caught this habit from their extraordinary teacher. 'I keep a book,' she declared later as she showed me a treasured, battered red leather

---

treasure trove of 'sayings' (and their derivations) and unusual words, 'so they all keep their own "word" and "sayings" books'. 'Sometimes', she smiled, 'I share one of my collection with them.'

Their teacher – the magician with the red leather book – had an extract from a football report in the local evening paper. She read the piece to the class and discussed, by using clever distributed, interactive and well-paced questions, the 'squad', the 'keeper', the 'Claret and Blues', 'relegation', 'Premier', and 'Europe'.

It all seemed on the surface run of the mill and yet the class, even to my untrained eye, had a sense of eager anticipation. 'Yes Class 6 what time is it?'

'It's question time,' they exclaimed. Without more ado they dispersed into groups – two teams of two pupils for each of the usual seven question words that all teachers use: when, why, which, who, where, what and how. Against a set time frame they were about to busy themselves in finding questions from the newspaper text. But before they did, their teacher asked them for something more. 'Don't forget Class 6 I shall want second and third frame questions . . . what are second frame questions . . . yes Craig?'

'Questions you can "infer" from the text, but aren't in it Miss?'

'Excellent Craig, and third frame questions Shakita?'

'Questions of hypothesis Miss,' replied Shakita.

'And then what shall we do?'

'We'll ask what we would do to test the hypothesis, Miss.'

And then the class were at work, also charged with pulling out at least two questions of grammar, punctuation and spelling from the text.

We think that the whole teaching process can be likened to a golden cracker. In the golden cracker there are essentially three parts. The first involves getting to know the youngsters – their likes and dislikes, their hopes and ambitions, their strengths and weaknesses and their preferred learning styles. The second and central part of the cracker involves a child practising skills, doing exercises, being occupied gainfully in consolidation of learning, whilst the teacher becomes proficient at classroom control and involved in the refined arts of planning and organisation. The third and most vital end of the cracker is the teacher's extraordinary skill as an alchemist of the mind, endlessly surprising children into doing and understanding things they never thought they could do. At this end lies the golden cusp of the teacher's skill: her or his ability to open the mind, often a part of teaching which is least analysed and discussed. It is particularly connected to the skills of questioning and speculating for pupils with different sorts of intelligences and at different stages of self-esteem, as illustrated in the example above.

The promotion of self-esteem is absolutely vital to the teaching and learning process. Michael Barber, in his book *The Learning Game*, explores the complex relationship between pupil self-esteem and teacher expectations in the form of a diagram (see Figure 3.1).

| | | Self Esteem | |
		Low	High
Expectations	**Low**	Failure	Complacency
	High	Demoralisation	Success

Figuere 3.1 The relationship between pupil self-esteem and teacher expectations
Source: Michael Barber, *The Learning Game*, 1996, p. 183

The most deadly combination is of course low self-esteem and low expectations leading inevitably to failure. However, if teachers have high expectations and the pupils still have low self-esteem there will be demoralisation; conversely if teachers have low expectations where the pupils enjoy high self-esteem there will be complacency. Success will come from promoting self-esteem and high expectations simultaneously, but this is very demanding and something that teachers need to work together to achieve.

It is from teachers we like and respect that we learn most readily.

If they are to achieve success the choice of tasks and targets and questions for learners clearly has to be based on varying pupil abilities and aptitudes, reflecting a differentiated approach. The successful school's overall teaching and learning policy will reflect Howard Gardner's theory of multiple intelligences set out in his book *The Unschooled Mind*, which sets out a minimum of seven distinct intelligences: logical–mathematical, linguistic, spatial, bodily-kinaesthetic, musical, interpersonal and intrapersonal.

It is the task of the planning groups to plan appropriate learning experiences for pupils so that all talents can be unlocked and all pupils achieve their full potential. This is a very exacting task, something that requires the collaborative skills and talents of all teachers in the planning and assessment process and is at the heart of an advanced teaching and learning culture.

> Whilst educators have always noted differences among learners, they have always been strongly inclined to believe that all students learn in similar ways. This assumption works out well . . . for those whose background and learning styles happen to be compatible with the teaching styles of their teachers, and for those who can learn in the way in which materials have traditionally been taught (say, from

teaching or text books). But there are also casualties: students who are motivated to learn but whose own learning styles or profiles of intelligence are not in tune with prevailing instructional practices.

(Howard Gardner, *The Unschooled Mind*, 1993, p. 244)

The introduction of the National Curriculum has caused all staff to be fully involved in the formal assessment of pupils' achievement and progress, and to plan with assessment in mind. This provides an opportunity for staff to work collaboratively on diagnostic assessment so that they understand the specific learning strengths or difficulties that pupils have, and to adjust content and approaches through formative assessment. Further, the statutory requirement for schools to set targets in literacy and numeracy for Year 6 and also for Year 11 in terms of five A–C grades, point scores, and the percentage of pupils with one GCSE pass or above has increasingly developed the shared understanding of attainment data, benchmarking and teacher forecasts for individual pupils, classes and year groups. Summative assessment will demonstrate how well pupils have performed and whether the teaching practices are effective or not, which, in turn, will lead to critical reflection on the teaching and learning policies adopted.

The effective use of learning resources

Twenty-first-century adults being taught by twentieth-century teachers in nineteenth-century classrooms

This is the great challenge schools face. The use and management of resources is integral to any discussion about teaching and learning, although resources on their own will not bring about real change in the classroom. There are key policy issues that need to be worked through concerning the use of resources, including teaching and learning styles, differentiation, the development of information skills, individual access to information technology, classroom management, and the role of the library/resource centre. The long-term development of pupil responsibility and independent learning requires an institutional approach, as does the development of the role of the teacher in managing resource-based learning. Increasingly, teachers need to be seen as managers of learning and less as presenters of information. In this context the use and management of classroom resources are fundamental to the extension of the range and repertoire of teachers' skills, whether it will be whole-class work, group work or independent learning.

Improving schools will have a medium- and long-term strategy on the place of information technology and computer-assisted learning across the curriculum, which will increase the ratio of computers to learners, enhance the expertise and confidence of the staff and improve access for all learners. When pupils come to school they leave the wired-up world of their homes where access to television, video, CD stereos and computers is commonplace, to enter a building where these resources for learning are still relatively few in number and not extensively employed in everyday teaching and learning. The old technologies of teaching and learning – talk, chalk, black/whiteboards and textbooks – are still dominant and the new technologies are only slowly making headway. Clearly, in a society and economy where information technology is transforming the way we live and earn our living, schools need to radically re-examine how pupils should be learning, not least because of all we know now about how pupils learn at different rates and in different ways. Computers are powerful tools for working towards the problem-solving skills that students will need in the workplace of the future as well as enhancing co-operative learning. Schools of the new millennium will have a vision of how to use shared intelligence rather than relying solely on teacher intelligence, although they will never forget that good teaching is a profoundly emotional activity borne out of perception, intuition and creative impulse.

In order for the teacher to manage and extend learning, schools should give particular thought to equipping every classroom with new technologies such as a 'teaching wall' containing television and video, together with computers and printers to facilitate independent learning. In such a way the use of information technology would become an integral part of curriculum planning. Once classrooms are equipped for accessing a range of information the role and function of the library/resource area and computer suites can be more clearly defined as part of the whole-school's approach to flexible learning. Full use of the new learning technologies helps the teacher to create an environment where pupils can build connections and create knowledge, something that can be carried on within the home and community, whereby computers in schools, libraries, other public buildings and potentially the home all have access to a common set of networked resources.

The National Grid for Learning will be a way of finding and using on-line learning and teaching materials. It will also help users to find their way around the wealth of content available over the Internet. Networks of learners and schools can be organised across the community, the country and the world. For example, some 40 Birmingham schools are already linked to sister schools in Chicago on the Internet, whereby teachers and pupils can talk to each other about different aspects of the curriculum and teaching and learning. Some other schools are already piloting universal e-mail address provision and this is a good way of getting home to pupils the new opportunities technology is opening up for communicating across borders and continents.

Learning through information and communication technologies (ICT) will enhance and enrich the curriculum, offering new and exciting opportunities for teachers to share and discuss best practice with each other and with experts, and for individual learners to access a wider range of quality learning programmes and materials. An improving school will take full advantage of the fact that both pupils and teachers can create, receive, collect, and share data, text, images and sounds on a vast range of topics, in ways more stimulating, richer and more timely than ever before if they have access to the appropriate technology and the will and ability to use it.

Monitoring and evaluation/collective review

Support with pressure is at the heart of classroom craft.

The quality of teaching is the major factor of school provision that makes a difference to pupils' achievements. It is only by holding teaching and learning up to review that schools identify the actual strengths and weaknesses that set the agenda for improvement. Every teacher should be able to examine and reflect on their own practice against agreed criteria and then be able to effectively monitor and reflect with other colleagues through a process that includes classroom observation. Sometimes this will be part of an effective appraisal scheme which provides for systematic monitoring and support but it could be an accepted part of ongoing self-evaluation and review. Evaluation will come from the will to collect evidence and debate implications, and it may be that the school adopts different strategies as a result of such feedback. The following are a set of practices that schools could use collaboratively to monitor and evaluate teaching and learning so that they are able to improve. They could:

- jointly review achievement data to analyse trends and make comparisons in order to set appropriate targets
- scrutinise pupils' work – sample books, folders, portfolios – across the ability range and years against set criteria
- review the quality of marking against assessment criteria and how effectively assessment is used to inform teaching
- observe teaching against set criteria such as evidence of effective methods and organisational strategies, high expectations and the skills of asking relevant questions and providing explanations
- review the learning environment, for example display, classroom organisation, storage and retrieval systems
- investigate the use of resources and their impact on learning, for example ICT across the curriculum; the use of textbooks and published schemes
- review the setting of homework (procedures, type and range) and how it reinforces and extends learning
- interview and survey pupils with reference to their learning experiences and their attitudes to learning
- interview and survey teachers, parents and governors using the same quality profile on teaching and learning
- analyse schemes of work/planning for the quality and range of curriculum delivery
- investigate particular aspects of teaching such as the beginning and

ending of lessons and the quality of differentiation, as part of action research

For example, one primary school had reviewed the way that lessons began and ended, and had concluded that if all pupils had classroom jobs for which they had applied the organisation of teaching and learning would be greatly enhanced, as in the following example.

The teacher ended her lesson in an everyday way, but with pace and subtlety. The tidying-up process was necessarily quick, but in its way as impressive as anything else for its familiar simplicity and brilliantly straightforward execution. Clearly the teacher had assigned ('well, that's not actually true, they apply for them,' she declared) tasks to each and every pupil to assist with classroom organisation, management, leadership and their collective life. So as a part of that, at the end of the lesson, on her downward count from 10 to 0, they moved silently, carefully and speedily, clearing and tidying to proud perfection.

It is clear that monitoring and evaluation is essential to effective teaching and learning in the classroom and that schools need to make sure that they have developed appropriate processes and practices which are thought through and implemented collectively. At its best, evaluation and review will be built into the everyday practices of teaching and learning, reinforced by a culture of constant staff talk and reflection based upon agreed criteria.

It would be useful for schools to apply this model continuously, and the more that schools can build systematic monitoring and evaluation into their everyday practice of teaching and learning, reinforced by constant staff task and discussion, the greater the impetus there will be to improving practice and raising the achievement of pupils.

Professional development

Good schools grow good teachers.

Improving schools are learning organisations in which everybody is engaged in the understanding and development of effective practice. Teachers teach, but they also have to be advanced learners in order to develop new skills and insights. It is the personal and professional growth of teachers that will have the most impact on pupil development. The new teacher joining the school will be somewhere on the continuum from beginning teacher to expert teacher, and it is essential that the received culture of teaching and learning is flexible and dynamic enough to take the teacher forward. Above all, our new teacher should feel that they are joining a school where staff are able and willing to scrutinise their practice and make this practice available to others, and where everybody tries to improve against their previous best. Staff development and school improvement are intimately related in the sense that they increase a school's capacity and performance, particularly if they are grounded upon a collaborative culture of values, beliefs and policies. There are four aspects of the teacher as learner which must be seen in combination:

- the improvement of skills
- the capacity to analyse and reflect on practice
- the ability to investigate, explore and collect evidence
- the confidence to receive and give ideas and assistance

It is the right of every teacher to observe teaching and be observed, as a collaborative activity distinct from the appraisal process, so that teachers can teach others the craft of teaching and reflect on practice together. This is part of the development of a collaborative teaching culture where everybody is a staff developer, gaining confidence from mutual observation in the form of confirming their strengths and improving weaker aspects of their practice.

School improvement is most surely and thoroughly achieved when:

- Teachers engage in frequent, continuous and increasingly precise *talk* about teaching practice . . . building up a shared language adequate to the complexity of teaching
- Teachers frequently *observe* each other teaching and provide each other with useful feedback
- Teachers *plan*, design, evaluate and prepare teaching materials together
- Teachers *teach each other* the practice of teaching
    (Judith Little, *The Power of Organisational Setting*, 1981)

As part of staff development in a successful school there will be coaching and mentoring involving pairs or small groups of staff working together. We are familiar with the role of mentor as applied to new or beginning teachers, but less familiar with the concept as applied to other staff. Clearly there are issues around the training and selection of mentors within a school, but once these have been talked through, the mentor system enhances the capacity of the staff to move forward. Coaching programmes are even less developed for staff but they often represent the best chance to implement teaching and learning improvements that impact upon pupil achievement. Coaching gets beyond teacher talk and the sharing of ideas to the specific enhancement of skills. The most common example would be developing the capacity of staff to use information technology in their teaching practices, but other examples would involve better use of questioning to access pupils' knowledge and challenge their thinking, and the effective use of ability grouping.

Roland Barth, in his book *Improving Schools from Within* (1990), writing about the school as a community of learners, refers to the instructions given by flight attendants to airline passengers: 'For those of you travelling with small children, in the event of an oxygen failure, first place the oxygen mask on your own face and then – and only then – place the mask on your child's face.' He goes on to comment:

> In schools we spend a great deal of time placing oxygen masks on other people's faces while we ourselves are suffocating. Principals, preoccupied with expected outcomes, desperately want teachers to breathe in new ideas, yet do not themselves engage in visible, serious learning. Teachers badly want their students to perform yet seldom reveal themselves to children as learners.
>
> (p. 42)

In such a professional culture one would also expect to see opportunities for debate on teaching and learning built into every staff meeting. For example, if staff meetings were sometimes held in classrooms in primary and special schools or in subject suites in secondary schools the host teacher(s) could be expected to spend 20 minutes explaining the classroom organisation, the learning environment, the use of resources and the range of teaching and learning strategies employed. Such a programme would give a powerful impetus to the centrality of teaching and learning, and if all staff subscribed to a common teaching and learning policy this would assist the dialogue in terms of debating within a shared, common language interpreted through specific classroom or subject teaching.

Everyone is a staff developer for everyone else.

Clearly, in terms of professional development all schools have five training days a year at their disposal to work as a whole staff, as well as directed time, and these days need to be very carefully tailored not only to the school development plan and action plan targets, but to the refinement of teaching and learning policies and practices in the light of collective evidence and experience. However, successful schools will often use other opportunities to create an ongoing professional development programme. The appraisal process could be more clearly identified with improvements in practice and opportunities for future professional development such as visits to other schools, attending specific conferences and opportunities for further study. The importance of ownership by teachers of their own professional development is vital, as it is a powerful trigger for increasing motivation and the capacity for innovation. Increasingly, groups of teachers from the same school are enrolling on masters degrees in school development which are taught partly on the school premises and enable participants to work as a team, discussing their work and ways to approach course material. Ideally, all members of staff would have an annual learning plan which would improve their skills and assist them on the journey towards greater expertise. Such a learning plan might look like the example below.

Annual learning plan

Work shadowing, for example other teachers within the school such as the deputy head, the literacy co-ordinator or the special needs co-ordinator.

Developing skills, for example using particular aspects of information technology in teaching, learning to use questioning more effectively, learning to differentiate more precisely.

Learning experiences, for example leading a task group and reporting findings, undertaking some action research, leading a parents' group on some aspect of the curriculum.

Learning targets, for example to attend specific courses and conferences, to read the research literature around a particular aspect of teaching and learning, to write an article for publication, to achieve a further qualification.

The work of establishing a strong collaborative culture around teaching and learning centres on the concept of the learning teacher who takes both informal and formal professional development very seriously as an integral and consistent part of their working life. Without the building of this culture individual initiatives to promote better teaching and learning will struggle to survive. The key question must always be, 'What can I do individually and collectively in my school to raise the standard of teaching and learning?'

Action research

In an effective teaching culture there will be an expectation that teachers and other staff carry out action research, either individually and collectively, and disseminate their findings so that practice is continually monitored and improved. Teachers are natural researchers, in the sense that all teaching is based on inquiry and the response of the pupils provides ready evidence as to the effectiveness of various teaching and learning approaches. Most teachers whilst in the act of teaching mentally check whether the groupings are working, whether the responses used are appropriate, whether the planned activities are appropriate to the needs of the class. Such pieces of active research commissioned around collective issues of teaching and learning in the particular context of the school would add immensely to the school's knowledge of what worked and didn't work and provide the evidence to make adjustments to policies and practices. This research could be done as part of a school–higher education link and therefore accredited or it could take place on a smaller level, as part of everyday practice. Clearly, even good schools are not successful for all pupils, and it would be important to identify from formative and summative assessment those groups that are not experiencing success in their learning. In certain learning activities and subjects boys are falling well behind girls. Does the school know exactly why this is? What is it doing to find out? Why is it that certain minority ethnic groups are underachieving? How can the school rectify this? What targets have been set to raise achievement for these groups? All teachers need to develop the capacity to research their practice and that of their colleagues so that they are able to promote school improvement and raise pupil achievement.

A primary school's action research programme for one year (teaching and learning)

- Two teachers and two learning assistants investigating a baseline assessment programme for groups of children with English as an additional language in partnership with parents.
- Two teachers researching accelerated learning techniques in Maths in Years 5 and 6.
- The IT postholder and deputy headteacher examining the impact of the Success Maker and Global programs in improving the basic skills of particular groups of pupils in Years 3 and 4.
- The headteacher and English postholder, with one teacher from each year and two learning assistants, benchmarking the planning, teaching and assessment of English with two other schools in the same family group.

Schools need to go further than this and publish their action research annually so that the debate can be taken further with other like-minded schools in the local consortia or across the LEA. In Birmingham, schools are divided into 'family groups' based upon such indicators as the percentage of free school meals, pupils with English as an additional language, pupil turnover and school size and they are encouraged to compare their assessment outcomes, particularly around literacy and numeracy in the primary school and subjects in the secondary school. An important consequence of this is that certain schools can be seen to be making a greater difference or adding greater value. The provision of individual school Performance and Assessment Reports (PANDAs) adds a greater impetus to find out how and why certain schools are doing better in terms of pupil achievement and therefore to set annual school targets that are already being achieved by some schools in the same group. Unless schools publish their action research it is difficult to start the dialogue of improving teaching and learning. Just as teachers need to be intellectually curious, so do schools as a whole.

Action research works best when it involves groups or the whole teaching staff working together. This shared process of collective investigation and review builds its own stimulus and energy in terms of analysing results and planning future developments, and guarantees the successful implementation of change. Intervention strategies, in terms of schools' participating in innovation and research, are referred to in Chapter 4.

Community involvement in the learning school

Although the school may have developed a strong teaching culture with appropriate attention to the various styles and forms of learning, outside forces may still undo some of this work unless it is reinforced by harnessing parents and the community to the task. Schools don't exist in a vacuum hermetically sealed from the outside. Indeed, the school day and school year provide only a small percentage of available learning time. To succeed in their hope of enhancing the teaching and learning process, schools must find new allies and build new sorts of connections to the community of which they are a part. One of the first key steps is to build an effective home and community curriculum, based mainly on learning partnerships with parents and carers, remembering that they are co-educators of children in parallel with teachers. Some of the following features of such a partnership would strengthen the capacity of the school to provide effective learning:

- home–school contracts to support learning at home in co-operation with the school, which may involve particular partnership schemes such as sending books or work home, lending libraries for toys and books for younger pupils or homework diaries for older pupils
- consultation twice a year with the parents and pupils, with the report as a *starting point* rather than a finishing point, to plan the next phase of pupils' learning with parental support
- a termly class meeting in primary schools to explain to parents the nature of the coming term's curriculum and how parents can reinforce this at home (backed up by written materials)
- good information provided about the school and about pupils' work and progress

- thematic parent's evenings or open weeks around such topics as the teaching of reading and numeracy or the use of information technology, at which parents can understand and participate in the learning process involved and support their children appropriately
- celebrating success through exhibitions, displays of pupils' achievements, and performances
- opportunities provided by the school for parents to enhance their own learning, sometimes gaining formal access qualifications, for example communication skills, parenting skills, health and safety education, information technology or to learn with their children such as family literacy schemes
- parents and community members becoming involved in the teaching and learning process as learning assistants or integration assistants (paid or voluntary) working alongside teachers

Other important agencies of community involvement which support teaching and learning include a wide range of organisations, service and businesses through which pupils can gain a greater economic understanding, an awareness of the world of work and of the nature of citizenship.

Businesses can contribute support, in terms both of skilled and committed employees and of sponsorship. Some schools are linked to businesses who provide mentors for pupils, to help raise their self-esteem and achievement. Other business volunteers help schools with their Young Enterprise programmes and work through Education Business Partnerships. Similarly, the careers service can be used to help raise the aspirations, motivation and achievements of young people. Links with local public libraries are a further boost to teaching and learning through homework and independent study.

Many schools are already established as community schools where the school buildings and facilities are used for the educational development of the whole community. However, all schools need to give fresh encouragement for local networks of providers and partners so that the collective energy of the community can boost the achievements of children and young people within the framework of a home, school and community curriculum.

Curriculum enrichment and extension

Good schools and good teachers are crucial to pupils' learning – yet effective teaching is not enough.

Success for young people also relies upon the homework and self-directed learning that they do out of school hours and classroom learning flourishes when good teaching and self-directed learning meet.

(John MacBeath, quoted in DfEE, *Extending Opportunity*, 1998, p. 8)

The most important attribute that schools can give pupils is the ability to learn on their own and to take responsibility for their own learning. Whilst this can be encouraged through the formal curriculum in terms of flexible learning and independent learning, the provision of curriculum enrichment and extension opportunities provides a real opportunity to prepare for lifelong learning. Extra-curricular provision is defined in a DfEE report:

- Curriculum enrichment: traditional extra-curricular activities such as sport, drama, chess, photography and other clubs and societies.
- Curriculum extension: study opportunities provided before or after school or during the breaks in the school day, such as homework clubs, extra revision classes and extra after-school tuition, whether undertaken voluntarily or as the result of teacher direction.
- Homework: work set in lessons, integral to the curriculum, to be done either at home or in curriculum extension time at school.

(DfEE, *School Performance and Extra Curricular Provision*, 1997)

A further DfEE publication in 1998, entitled *Extending Opportunity: A national framework for study support*, defines study support as 'learning activity outside normal lessons which young people take part in voluntarily'. This framework is intended to help all those who play a part as providers working with children and young people

Different schools in different phases will make extra-curricular provision to promote learning experiences. Certainly, the provision of homework is seen by many schools and parents as a valuable and essential part of school work and forms part of many home–school agreements, with homework diaries being reviewed by teachers and parents. Schools need to carefully research the provision, range and type of homework set and, above all, be consistent in their practice in both setting it and taking it back. As with the provision of curriculum enrichment and extension, homework should be part of a coherent, whole-school policy on teaching and learning.

Characteristic of good practice in curriculum enrichment and extension are the monitoring of pupil involvement by age, gender and race, opportunities for individual self-study before, during and after school, the involvement of a large proportion of staff and the provision of a wide variety of types of activity to encourage participation by as many pupils as possible. Many Birmingham secondary schools have been able to develop an impressive range of study support, including homework clubs, breakfast clubs, subject surgeries, study weeks, help with key skills, Easter revision programmes for Year 11 pupils, summer literacy schools, and the use of a range of volunteers to offer one-to-one support (referred to in Chapter 4). Similarly, primary schools have developed 'Early Birds' schemes for children who want or need to be in school early, stay-late clubs, study extension with the Children's University, family learning and residential activities. The Birmingham Primary Guarantee specifically sets out a set of learning experiences which in part depend upon extended study opportunities, such as a residential experience for all children.

Curriculum enrichment and extension allows for a greater flexibility of teaching and learning, particularly around techniques such as accelerated learning and concepts such as multiple intelligence. There are also extra opportunities for developing information and communication technology skills. Above all, an improving school will provide these opportunities to improve motivation, build self-esteem, develop effective learning and raise achievement.

Study-support activity strengthens pupils' overall achievements in the main curriculum.

The celebration of teaching and learning

Our new teacher joining the school would become a better teacher just by being on the staff if there was a culture sustaining quality teaching and learning. In such a culture teaching would be a joyful experience with a staff full of energy creators showing infectious enthusiasm and commitment, and pupils and adults alike would be engaged as active learners encouraging everyone else's learning. The staff would celebrate their successes through their staffroom talk, through their shared language in planning meetings and through their intellectual curiosity as they debated the best ways to improve their practice.

The *Times Educational Supplement* has for some time had a weekly column on the subject of 'My Best Teacher', and it is interesting to reflect upon the qualities that are most often commented on by past pupils. The articles re-affirm the joy of teaching and learning and remind us all that we can instantly recall from our own experience the teachers who were enthusiastic, committed and caring, who treated everyone fairly, and who were interested in us as individuals. We remember our best teachers as those who made learning exciting, were good communicators, were very willing to help and obviously enjoyed their jobs. We also recall their spontaneity, humour and mannerisms. Above all, we remember them as passionate teachers who liked kids, loved learning and had the capacity to touch our hearts.

Robert Fried argues, in his book *The Passionate Teacher*, that for teachers 'passion is not just a personality trait that some people have and some others lack, but rather something discoverable, teachable, and reproducible, even when the regulations of school life gang up against it. Passion and practicality are not opposing notions; good planning and design are as important as caring and spontaneity in bringing out the best in students.'

The qualities and characteristics of good teachers have been listed by Michael Barber and Tim Brighouse as follows:

Good teachers, qualities and characteristics
- Good understanding of self and of interpersonal relationships
- Generosity of spirit
- Sense of humour
- Sharp observational powers
- Interest in and concern for others
- Infectious enthusiasm for what is taught
- Imagination
- Energy
- Intellectual curiosity
- Professional growth and understanding of how children learn
- Ability to plan appropriate learning programmes for particular classes/groups/individuals
- Understanding of their curriculum in the context of the school as a whole

(Michael Barber and Tim Brighouse,
Partners in Change: Enhancing the Teaching Profession, 1992)

In the school there would be a generosity of spirit as expert teachers mentored and coached other teachers and an opportunity for all teachers to lead the debate at certain times. There would be a sense of success when teachers felt confident to talk with a supportive group about what they were learning to do better as well as what they did well. There would be a collective pride around belonging to the staff of such a school, reinforced by the achievements of pupils, the publication of action research and the recognition of individual and collective expertise beyond the school. It would be noticed by the new teacher that the school was often visited by other headteachers, teachers and advisers who would be eager to see at first hand the effectiveness of teaching and learning in the school and to participate further in the debate to make this even better.

> There is a striking quality to fine classrooms. Pupils are caught up in learning; excitement abounds; and playfulness and seriousness blend easily because the purposes are clear, the goals sensible, and an unmistakable feeling of well-being prevails. Artist teachers achieve these qualities by knowing both their subject matter and their pupils; by guiding the learning with deft control – a control that itself is born out of perception, intuition, and creative impulse.
>
> (Lou Rubin, *Artistry in Teaching*, 1985)

In terms of learning, a walk around the school would provide further opportunities to question, speculate and analyse. The classroom and all learning areas and spaces would make their contribution to the joy and excitement of the learning process. The rhythms of the school day and the school year would provide for enhanced teaching and learning opportunities and for learning and teaching celebrations. The school community would have clearly thought-out ideas on learning assemblies, opportunities for independent study in the library or particular resource areas, the development of study skills and the provision of one-to-one learning opportunities to overcome a learning difficulty or extend a learning talent. Information technology would enhance opportunities for pupils, teachers and parents to learn from each other as well as through particular programmes and the Internet. Curriculum extension and enrichment opportunities would provide for year-round learning through residential experiences or the opportunity to join other pupils in learning organisations providing after-school and vacation learning experiences. The school would endeavour to provide success for everyone – staff as well as pupils – by providing people with multiple entry points to success and opportunities to celebrate success.

We started this chapter by affirming that the quality of teaching and learning is at the heart of school improvement and we have described some processes and practices that would enable any school to secure continuous improvement in this area. In particular, we have stressed the importance of the establishment and development of an effective teaching and learning culture which is constantly being energised through staff and pupils taking responsibility to improve on their previous best. In this sense good schools are always in the making, taking their mission very seriously and developing their own internal dynamic related to:

- Unquenchable intellectual curiosity with reference to fields of knowledge and pedagogy
- A relentless press towards attaining higher standards of achievement for all pupils.
- A huge commitment to building confidence, competence and self-esteem among all learners
- Passionate teachers and staff, whose goal is always the highest quality of learning experiences for pupils

> Teaching is the vocation of vocations, because to choose teaching is to enable the choices of others. It is to be about the business of empowerment, the business of enabling others to choose well.
> (William Ayers, *To Teach, the Journey of a Teacher*, 1993)

If we take those particular feature of schools with successful teaching and learning policies and practices the central ingredient is that of collegiality among the staff promoting improved teaching practice and getting better results. These schools have more than competent individual staff. They have the organisational capacity to work productively as a group for high-quality learning for all pupils. Susan Rosenholtz's research in *Teachers' Workplace*, found collegiality to be the important element that differentiates 'learning enrichment' from 'learning improvement' schools. Teaching can be a lonely enterprise with the unremitting demands of the day taking precedence over long-term goals of improving practice. Collegiality and school culture are connected, in that teachers and colleagues work together with the triumphs of collective efforts outweighing the price of solitary struggles. Teaching and learning cultures have to be built and developed through induction, professional development, joint planning, coaching and mentoring, sharing good practice and researching the evidence. The bedrock of this culture are the norms, values and beliefs that bond a community of like-minded people into the common commitment of continually improving practice and raising standards of achievement for pupils.

Teachers affect eternity; they can never tell where their influence stops.

Duncan and Colin . . . the cause of exasperated despair to their teachers and their mothers alike

Duncan and Colin – these are not their real names – don't know each other but they have much in common. They are troublesome youngsters – a worry and the cause of exasperated despair to their teachers and their mothers alike. Both have been through periods when they have been more or less in school. Both are vulnerable and of course both are boys. Duncan must now be 12 going on 13. I caught sight of him not long ago in the labyrinth of streets in that bit of the city centre in Digbeth which reminds you of what Birmingham used to be like before it was transformed. I stopped the car to call after him but he was gone.

I had first met Duncan when he had been sent to sit outside the head's office in a Small Heath primary school. He was clearly in trouble but talked to me animatedly about 'the Blues' whom he never actually watched. He followed matches by listening to the roar while outside St Andrews as he 'looked after' supporters' cars and earned a little money in the process. 'He is a lovely boy,' confided the head, 'but he finds it impossible in a class of 30. So does his teacher and so do his classmates.' She continued, 'Mind you, he's really good at running errands and he's fine on a one-to-one basis, and is utterly reliable.' As if to prove it, she left him in charge of the office as we went around the school.

The head told me of Duncan's background, some of which she'd gathered, the rest learnt from the education social worker, whose lot is so often to spend time trying to pick up the pieces arising from human misery of one sort or another, while trying to strike a balance between understanding the family's need and giving priority to attendance at school which represents the only hope for the next generation.

Duncan was the eldest of three and his mum was always on the move, fleeing from the debt and violence in their lives – a private letting here, a women's refuge there. The ESW tried to keep track but reckoned – and the head agreed – Duncan would never make secondary school. He'd be lost to the system and his mum wouldn't insist. He'd take what education he experienced from the streets. That's why I stopped the car in Digbeth.

So if that's Duncan, what about Colin? It was another support worker – an educational psychologist – who told me his dilemma. Colin had been excluded from two primary schools because of his behaviour. Colin had been the victim of sexual abuse when he was younger and couldn't seem to learn how not to make explicit sexual remarks in the playground and in the corridor. His behaviour towards other children went far beyond the boisterous. The educational psychologist was picking up Colin just as his third school, not surprisingly, had said 'Enough is enough.' The case conference now suggested a placement in one of our schools for emotionally and behaviourally disturbed youngsters, but the place wouldn't be available for two terms. The educational psychologist then showed that precious but exhausting quality which distinguishes all really good public servants: she felt obligated, so she wouldn't let it rest. She knew the mother was at her wits' end and that the last thing Colin needed was two terms of his education at home or on the streets. On a half chance, she took Colin and his mother to a primary school which a colleague had recommended because the head and her staff were very unconventional. I know the school and I'd agree. On the journey back from the school Colin confided to nobody in particular 'I think they like me.' Sure enough, shortly afterwards the school decided to admit Colin. Two terms later he is indistinguishable from his classmates and as his teacher said, 'His behaviour and attitude are fine.'

Although Colin owes a great deal to the school, his teacher and the psychologist none of them are so romantic that they don't realise that when he changes school it might all go wrong again. So what, you might ask, are the lessons from the cases of Duncan and Colin?

First, of course, their lives bear witness both to the increased and often lonely turbulence which so many youngsters now face and to the sheer chance involved in meeting the right person which seems to determine life's chances for the most vulnerable. Second, beyond the school, the support services – here it was an educational social worker and an educational psychologist – have an often thankless task, attempting, as it were – or so it seems to them – to deal with casualties in a major traffic accident equipped only with a box of sticking plaster. We see and complain about the mistakes such workers make, generally from being too stretched, and overlook the minor miracles they sometimes perform by ingenuity and commitment.

Overwhelmingly, however, the cases of Duncan and Colin underline two things. The most vulnerable need a better organised response from us, as well as more resources. Second, we have a very long way to go before we really deliver on equal opportunity. That's very chastening for me, since I am keenly aware that ultimately it's my responsibility. In the meantime I cannot express my admiration sufficiently strongly for those – whether in schools or support services – who unlock the talents of youngsters like Colin and Duncan.

4

INTERVENTIONS

Change is the sum of a thousand acts of re-perception and behaviour at every level of the organisation.

(John Kao, *Jamming*, 1996)

Change comes from small initiatives which work, initiatives which imitated, become the fashion. We cannot wait for great visions from great people, for they are in short supply at the end of history. It is up to us to light our own small fires in the darkness.

(Charles Handy, *The Empty Raincoat*, 1994)

In previous chapters we have been attempting a kind of grammar of school improvement in which the nouns are the key factors of school effectiveness and the verbs the key processes of school improvement. We have also provided some adjectives in the form of descriptors of successful practices. However, to change the meaning of the sentences and paragraphs that make up the story of school improvement we need to look at the punctuation marks and the construction of the adverbial clauses. In particular, the subtleties are to be found in those small interventions or punctuations that have a disproportionate effect on meaning and change. We call these small interventions 'butterflies' after the work on chaos theory which has produced the concept of the 'butterfly effect'. This teaches us that tiny differences in input can quickly become overwhelming differences in output. In weather, for example, it is argued that butterflies stirring the air today in Peking can transform storm systems next month in New York.

The adverbial clauses of school improvement are those larger critical interventions which are part of an integrated and focused programme of change which may take up to a year to implement and perhaps longer to embed thoroughly in the culture of the school. They are part of the school's improvement strategy and reflect the deliberate actions taken by the school in order to plan for future development.

Taken together, the quality and scope of small and large interventions are critical success factors in sustaining the progress of school improvement, but *how* a school approaches the processes and interventions is critical too.

Butterflies

Butterflies are best described in the impact they have on the everyday life of the school and the processes of school improvement. In the first chapter those processes were described as teaching and learning, leadership, management and organisation, collective review, creating an environment, staff development and links with parents. The best butterflies will affect the most processes and make an immediate and disproportionate difference to the climate and culture of the school. Whilst schools might be putting into place some small changes as part of the continual educational review process there needs to be a deliberate strategy to collect butterflies so that they can be developed and shared effectively. There are a number of techniques that can enable this to happen, to make up the school butterfly effect.

The school butterfly effect

Describe and define what butterflies are to the staff and how they can effect change.

↓

Design an appropriate pro forma to capture the essence of these small interventions relating their effect to the seven processes of school improvement and their impact on changing practices.

↓

Initially ask all staff for three contributions that may affect teaching and learning practices.

↓

Publish these as a collection for dissemination and debate and decide on those to be collectively implemented.

↓

Build the collection of butterflies into the culture of the school by starting all staff meetings with the description of a butterfly, and asking for further contributions on specific themes such as raising achievement, and promoting a positive ethos.

↓

Extend the process to include governors and the wider school community.

↓

Evaluate the cumulative effect of these many small interventions on the effectiveness of the school.

↓

Continue to publish and disseminate collections of new butterflies whilst reviewing, and if necessary modifying, those that are already being practised.

Through this process the school will continue to put into practice a number of small interventions that are capable of transforming behaviour and practice but, most importantly, the staff will also be engaged in thinking, speculating and reflecting on the processes of school improvement and the subtleties of change.

Here follow some illustrations of butterflies that are known to have had a disproportionate effect on school improvement after being tried in many Birmingham schools.

Annual learning plans

Description

The staff of this school, including teachers, learning assistants, integration assistants and non-teaching staff wanted to show their commitment to learning and personal development in their ambition to create a true, learning school. Governors were also encouraged to participate. Accordingly they agreed to fill out on an annual basis a single pro forma which set out their learning targets in terms of knowledge and understanding, skills, reading, work shadowing and general professional development.

Processes involved

Teaching and learning
Creating an environment
Collective review
Staff development

Comment on impact

The staff felt appropriately challenged to set themselves personal learning targets and were pleased to share with each other their rate of progress. In some cases they relied on each other to develop certain skills (for example, those related to information technology) or acquire particular knowledge. When the learning plans were reviewed by a person of their choice they were delighted at their success. Some have now formalised their learning plans into obtaining further qualifications; altogether the school can justly say that with its pupils, parents and governors it is a learning community.

Developing the school's process for welcoming visitors

Description

A variety of pupils are selected to show visitors around the school and are given some preliminary training to agree on where they should go, what information needs to be given about the school and how they should conduct themselves. On each occasion, both visitors and guides are asked to complete an evaluation sheet about the visit. Good ideas and useful responses are recorded in a Visitors' Guide File for future use.

Processes involved

Creating an environment
Teaching and learning
Leadership

Comment on impact

Pupils take real pride in their school and become much more knowledgeable about it. They improve in their personal and social skills through meeting visitors and answering questions and are able to practise leadership. They gain in self-esteem in being trusted to guide visitors, getting positive feedback from the evaluations and in being part of the process of developing the school's strategy for welcoming visitors.

Noticing children: overcoming the invisible child

Description

The school was alarmed by NFER research (1992) which confirmed that many secondary school children can go through a term or more without having a serious conversation with a teacher about their progress. The school had decided on a scheme which you got to hear about if you attended the daily staff briefing . . . 'Today's children are Dean Sheffield in 7R and Ann Riley in 8S. You know the drill.' A member of staff explained the 'drill'. If you taught 7R or 8S you were to complete a report on what Dean Sheffield and Ann Riley did or didn't do during the lesson, on an agreed observation sheet. If anyone who didn't teach them saw either of them during lunchtime or in the corridors and noticed whom they were talking to, what they were doing or not doing, they were also expected to scribble a quick note. Completed forms and notes were to be given to the form tutor at the end of the school day. Reports on all children to be so identified were then to be passed on to year heads and to the head and deputies who were planning a follow-up review of the scheme.

Processes involved

Collective review
Staff development
Management and organisation

Comment on impact

The perception of need for the scheme had arisen out of a staff development committee. The school was familiar with John Gray's measurements of school success: academic performance, pupil commitment/attitude and satisfaction, a child having a worthwhile relationship with at least one member of the school staff. They were anxious to notice children who might be 'slipping through the net' as they put it. So the children were not chosen for study at random but were those whom form tutors believed that people knew least about. This initiative draws attention to the need for everyone to be known, and is particularly relevant in the context of a large school.

Improving staff meetings: changing venues and hosts

Description

A primary school decided to hold its weekly staff meetings in classrooms rather than the staffroom or library. Every teacher would host a staff meeting on a rota basis and the first item on the agenda would be an explanation by the teacher of the particular learning environment and how the classroom was organised.

Processes involved

Staff development
Creating an environment
Collective review
Teaching and learning
Management and organisation
Leadership

Comment on impact

Although somewhat apprehensive at first, teachers and learning assistants have found the process extremely useful in explaining and sharing ideas about classrooms and the organisation of learning. This collective-review process has helped teachers both to celebrate good practice and to improve against their previous best. The major topics which have been discussed concern classroom display, the organisation of learning resources, the layout of the room and the development of particular learning areas. This process has led to the formation of whole-school guidelines, a better appreciation of teaching and learning practice in the school, and an improved quality of classroom organisation and teaching.

Improved communication between governors and staff

Description

Governing body meetings are held in different parts of the school in order to communicate and celebrate the specific teaching and learning that goes on in departmental areas. The specialist staff host the meeting and explain the learning environment by conducting a tour of the facilities, making a short presentation and answering questions. This need only take 30 minutes before the meeting starts and it could be followed by a specific agenda item on the learning area concerned. Staff then attend the meeting as observers to learn about the work of the governing body.

Processes involved

Staff development
Management and organisation
Teaching and learning
Collective review

Comment on impact

Schools where this has been tried comment on the great gains it provides in terms of governors getting to know their school and their staff and appreciating different aspects of the curriculum and specific processes of teaching and learning. It also affects accommodation and budget decisions. Teachers gain from getting an opportunity of meeting all governors, explaining how they work and celebrating their good practice. It gives the governors a chance to be involved in a collective-review process which strengthens school development planning and decision taking. Communication and relationships between governors and staff improve considerably.

Appointing new teachers

Description

As part of the selection process, candidates are asked to teach a lesson before they are formally interviewed. They are told in advance what year and subject/topic they will be expected to teach and something about the ability range of the pupils. They are observed according to set criteria by one or two members of staff (not necessarily members of the interview panel) who take into account the views of pupils. The reports of the observer(s) are analysed and considered by the panel in the follow-up selection procedure.

Processes involved

Staff development
Management and organisation
Teaching and learning

Comment on impact

Recruitment of staff is one of the most important of management activities and it is therefore worth investing more care and time to select the best. Asking teachers to demonstrate their craft would seem to be a more effective way than relying solely on interview and references. It also has the benefit of involving other staff in the processes of classroom observation and staff selection, as well as involving the pupils. Decisions taken on appointing new teachers are thus more widely shared and probably more successful. The interviewees also gain from the process, in that it gives them a chance to find out more about what the school and its pupils are really like and to demonstrate skills that might not be revealed in the interview.

Transforming attitudes towards achievement:
The assembly strategy

Description

The headteacher was explaining to the assembled lower school the importance of effort and achievement. It was the beginning of a school year. 'When you look at your work in any subject, your teacher wants you to be making progress as well as consolidating what you know already. Of course it is important to practice . . . but the real prize is when you make the next step forward in your skill if it is at sport, or in your understanding academic work. But it is up to you to set targets for extending your skills in your subjects and, of course, your knowledge and understanding.' The headteacher then went on to explain how she and the three deputies would be helping children to do just that. At lower school assembly on Tuesdays, Wednesdays and Thursdays throughout the year, the four of them would be giving the names of four youngsters who would then bring their books – all their books – to them at break times on that particular day. 'So it is important you have thought about where you are in your subjects and that you pick out one thing which you are really proud of in your progress and another you would like to improve on with help. A sort of obstacle you can tell us about.'

Of course, the school accompanied this initiative with some careful planning among the tutors in Years 7, 8 and 9 and the year heads, so they too spent some time in tutorials preparing youngsters for the sort of discussions they might have with the senior management team.

Processes involved

Leadership
Collective review
Staff development
Teaching and learning
Parental involvement

Comment on impact

The virtues of this initiative include the head and the three deputies showing interest in 'teaching and learning'. It was also shared leadership, because the suggestion for the move had come from their form tutors who wanted work on day books (or Records of Achievement) to be given higher profile. It is hard to escape the conclusion that the school's marking policy would be given greater emphasis. Indeed, the senior management team said it was a less threatening way of establishing an examining consistency in that respect than the time-honoured one of heads calling in whole-class examples of books and marking. Moreover, during the year the senior management team would engage in meaningful conversations with 360 children in a lower school of 500. The school said it intended to keep it up to see if the outcomes later at 16-plus would be affected. They believed they would be. A further extension of the scheme was being considered – namely to send a personal letter, handwritten, at the end of the break period to the parents of the particular children concerned, to reinforce home–school partnerships.

Praise postcards

Description

When a pupil has done something that demonstrates improvement or merit a teacher fills in the details on a pre-designed school postcard which the headteacher signs and posts to the parents.

Processes involved

Leadership
Management and organisation
Teaching and learning
Parental involvement

Comment on impact

The use of these praise postcards has done a great deal to raise the self-esteem of many pupils. Parents have very much enjoyed receiving them and some have commented that when they previously received communications from the school they always expected it to be bad news. Staff have found them very easy to complete as the format is already established.

A staffroom teaching and learning noticeboard

Description

A special noticeboard is allocated in the staffroom just for articles, comments, cuttings, book reviews, butterflies, and so on related to teaching and learning. In one primary school all the staff take it in turn every two weeks to provide materials for the noticeboard and to talk about this during a staff meeting. In a secondary school subject departments provide the material every two weeks, but on general teaching and learning issues not just their subject discipline.

Processes involved

Staff development
Collective review
Teaching and learning
Creating an environment

Comment on impact

As it is placed in the staffroom the noticeboard does generate interest and discussion about teaching and learning informally and formally. These noticeboards usually highlight key articles from the *Times Educational Supplement*, education magazines and other sources, as well as books that would aid staff development. Sometimes there is also a 'butterfly of the week' displayed.

Young teachers' club

Description

Older primary pupils are trained to work with younger children in developing reading skills. This is one step on from traditional shared reading methods, as the children meet as a group to share ideas and problems, have a file in which they record their activities and comments and are expected to share time in school.

Year 6 children are invited to take part at the beginning of each term/year and a list is drawn up matching younger children. They are then allocated a time in the week, in this school's case always at ERIC time, when they go to share reading with their 'partners'. Meetings have to be arranged, as 'training' sessions are important and certainly raise their self image.

Processes involved

Teaching and learning
Creating an environment
Collective review
Management and organisation
Leadership

Comment on impact

The older children involved seem to have gained confidence from their involvement, talking about their own future in terms of teaching. The boys recognise that working with small children is valid, which must impact on their future role as parents. The smaller children gain from having a strong input and teachers are supported by having class work followed through.

Critical interventions

Success comes in cans; failure comes in can'ts.

We have previously defined these as integrated and focused programmes of educational activities which are designed to make a distinct difference to previous practice. They will usually have a significant impact on teachers' behaviour as reflective professionals, on pupil development and learning, and on whole-school culture, and they need to be monitored and evaluated appropriately. Critical interventions, as major case studies of educational change, form part of the action research of a school and ought to be written up and published as a demonstration of the school's commitment to being part of a learning community. It can often be the case that schools have introduced what may be termed critical interventions, but they have never been followed up effectively and their impact is at best limited to parts of the school and at worst is not recognised to have made any difference. In these times of schools facing their first or even second OFSTED inspections, it can be a salutary exercise for schools to be asked exactly what their critical interventions have been, and to what extent they have been successful and for whom. Further, is the evidence available to demonstrate that success?

To make critical interventions have a lasting impact, all schools will need to utilise the skills of particular people throughout the organisation, in particular those energy creators and teams who have the vision, commitment and relationships to conceptualise and plan the intervention, promote it and bring it to fruition.

There are we believe, some critical interventions which are more rather than less likely to increase success. These are set out in some detail below.

Extending achievement: levering up curriculum provision through benchmarking, using standards maps

Schools are continually seeking to extend achievements in particular areas or aspects of the curriculum, but find it difficult to establish a sense of progression. However, a school could establish a set of standards maps using criteria from OFSTED, the Qualifications and Curriculum Authority (QCA) and the LEA, which would illustrate the various stages of the journey of improvement. These could be benchmarked as follows.

At the *emergent* level the school has in place:

Stage 1   A few policies
Stage 2   Some practices, not all effective
Stage 3   Has yet to collect evidence systematically

At the *established* level the school has in place:

Stage 1   Policies
Stage 2   Some successful practices and achievements
Stage 3   The beginnings of a monitoring process which reflect increased effectiveness
Stage 4   Some changes to policies and practices, but often on opinion rather than systematic evaluation

At the *advanced* level the school has in place:

Stage 1   Policies
Stage 2   Mainly successful practices and achievements
Stage 3   Rigorous monitoring systems for practices
Stage 4   Regular reviews of practices in the light of evidence
Stage 5   Changes to practices/policies as a result of evaluation

These benchmarks could be applied to such areas/aspects as:

• literacy
• numeracy
• information technology
• the arts
• science
• sport
• community development
• personal and social education
• environmental education
• equal opportunities

Tables 4.1–4.7 show examples of a standards map for equal opportunities (EO) provision using these three levels and aligning them against the seven Birmingham processes of school improvement:

• teaching and learning
• leadership
• management and organisation
• collective review
• creating an environment
• staff development
• involvement of parents

A standard for equality of opportunity in schools

Table 4.1 Equality of opportunity in teaching and learning

Emergent	Established	Advanced
Some curriculum policies address equality issues and there is good practice within the school.	All curriculum policies address equality of opportunity and implementation is monitored.	Curriculum themes and vocational programmes actively promote EO policy.
Some teachers make use of pupils' own knowledge, culture or experience in their teaching.	School decides to run additional extra-curricular activities to encourage under-represented groups.	EO issues are explored with pupils, e.g. in work that examines fact, opinion and stereotyping. Pupils have systematic opportunities to acquire life skills, e.g. parenting, assertiveness.
School recognises and celebrates festivals of different cultures/religions.	Assemblies for year are planned to include focus on achievement by people from different ethnic groups/gender/disability.	'Celebrations' are regularly geared towards race, gender, disability themes and inter-faith tolerance. Pupil participation is encouraged and monitored.
There is a policy addressing the specific language needs of pupils for whom English is an additional language.	There are whole-school practices addressing the language needs of pupils for whom English is an additional language.	School communicates effectively with pupils and parents for whom English is an additional language.
	Awards evenings celebrate a wide range of achievement and are planned to promote the EO policy.	Guidance is written for staff and other adults on use of any materials with bias.

Table 4.2 Equality of opportunity in leadership

Emergent	Established	Advanced
Headteacher discusses with staff the stereotypical bias in children's work and some displays in school; achievements of women and minority ethnic groups are on display.	All staff share goals about learning, behaviour and relationships and have high expectations of all pupils.	Practice in promoting equality of opportunity is consistent throughout the school.
Headteacher has asked governing body to consider equality of opportunity as an issue for the school. Senior management team has decided to present paper to staff meeting on implementing equality of opportunity.	All staff, including midday supervisors, are involved in drawing up and monitoring policy.	Headteacher, with governing body, analyses budget to ensure pupils with different needs receive appropriate share of resources available.

Table 4.3 Equality of opportunity in management and organisation

Emergent	Established	Advanced
School has a policy, some practices and there is a statement in the school prospectus.	School has policy and established practices for equality of opportunity, including practices to deal with racial/sexual harassment/abuse.	Has fully integrated policy for EO in curriculum and employment, linked to development plan targets.
A member of staff has been designated as the equal opportunities co-ordinator.	EO and anti-bullying policies are actively promoted.	Consideration is given to grouping of pupils within and across classes to promote equality of opportunity.
The governing body has nominated a governor to be responsible for equality of opportunity.	Governing body's composition is monitored for reflection of school's community.	Structures clearly indicate from whom pupils may seek advice and support on EO matters.
Consideration, adoption and extension of LEA/city council policy. School has a non-racist, non-sexist dress code.	There is regular review of EO policies and practice. Race, gender and disability equality form part of employment policy; school monitors outcomes and ensures emergency lists enable school to reflect better balance of staff.	Policy and practice are reviewed every two years in light of changing profile re gender, ethnicity and disability. Evidence informs school development plan priorities with appropriate budget allocation.
Headteacher has plans to report to governing body on gender/ethnicity in staffing profile.	Headteacher reports regularly to governing body on EO issues.	Headteacher reports regularly to governing body and LEA on progress in implementing equality of opportunity.

Table 4.4 Equality of opportunity in the collective review process

Emergent	Established	Advanced
Senior management team monitors certain trends, e.g. numbers of exclusions or achievements of boys, and begins to review reasons for these.	School monitors trends, including academic results, by ethnicity and gender. Senior management team sets targets for different ethnic groups and for girls and boys.	School evaluates and sets annual targets for improved performance and participation by under-performing groups. Parents are involved. Action plans outline strategies to achieve this.
Some subject departments and primary co-ordinators monitor the performance of different ethnic groups and girls/boys.	School moderates achievement levels with school with similar gender/ethnic/socio-economic intake.	School uses older pupils and students in training to help monitor and evaluate practice.
Audit of library by individuals for examples of bias in gender, ethnicity, disability.	EO criteria set for purchase of all resources to achieve better balance and teaching targets.	Resources regularly monitored by staff and pupils and EO criteria amended as required.
	School surveys pupil satisfaction/commitment/ opinion along with bullying/racial/sexual harassment experiences and shares outcomes with all staff.	Practices for dealing with complaints include student involvement at appropriate stages.

Table 4.5 Equality of opportunity in the school environment

Emergent	Established	Advanced
Occasional displays of non-stereotypical material.	School mounts exhibitions to emphasise positive role models, e.g. achievements of females from a variety of ethnic groups, particularly in management and science, achievements of males in the arts and caring professions.	Systematic checks for 'institutional prejudice', e.g. use of language/distribution of awards, authority figures. Pupils, with staff support, organise their own groups such as school councils, where equality issues can be raised and discussed.

Table 4.6 Equality of opportunity in staff development

Emergent	Established	Advanced
Whole-staff discussions on equality of opportunity have taken place and further training is planned.	INSET (including contributors) is planned to reinforce the EO commitment to the school (including debate on achievement in the context of ethnicity, gender, disability, deprivation factors). *All* staff involved.	EO objectives are part of staff development, appraisal. All the staff's personal learning plans for the year include an element of extending their knowledge and skill in equality of opportunity.

Table 4.7 Equality of opportunity in parental/community involvement

Emergent	Established	Advanced
There has been a governing body discussion on access for disabled pupils.	School has reviewed and monitored access for pupils with disabilities and has action plan for improvement as resources allow.	Environment is fully accessible to people with disabilities.
	Use is made of individuals and groups from the local community and beyond to provide expertise and positive role models, e.g. artists in residence schemes, Women in Management.	School employs associate teachers and other adults to provide role models. Professional role model scheme operates with volunteers.
	School provides facilities for local community.	Parents and community groups consulted on effectiveness of EO policy. School ensures views of under-represented groups are sought systematically on key school issues.
		School has partnership with community groups, e.g. supplementary schools to promote achievement of particular groups.

The information gained from the benchmarking shown in Tables 4.1–4.7 would give the school a means of improving its curriculum provision and extend professional reflection as well as pupil development and achievement. If the benchmarks were more widely shared across schools there would be a huge impetus to professional development through visits to schools where provision was benchmarked as 'advanced'. There would be an incentive to make appropriate progression and achieve an improved standard validated through specialist review committees (either internal or external through the LEA). A school that achieved an 'advanced' benchmark would be given an opportunity to celebrate its success on a wider stage and develop centres of excellence shared by other schools, the community, the LEA and nationally.

Critical steps

- establish criteria and standards as benchmarks
- audit present curriculum provision against those standards
- create opportunities to extend and develop practices and policies
- establish review teams to monitor practices and award standards
- celebrate success and develop best practice even further

Turning up the power: providing one-to-one learning opportunities when a child needs them

All children are gifted . . . some just open their
packages sooner than others

We know that pupils will benefit considerably from having a programme of one-to-one tutoring, coaching, mentoring or other support at critical moments in their school life, which usually involve overcoming a learning difficulty or extending a particular capability. However, schools have often not reviewed the range of opportunities provided in this way as a means of meeting every pupil's needs, and some pupil-tracking of teaching and learning provision may well reveal ineffective distribution of such extra teaching resources as the school has. It would be useful to conduct an audit of the current situation and to plan a way forward in expanding one-to-one learning opportunities. Most schools will have learning assistants and there is considerable scope here to both increase this provision and focus more effectively on the needs of particular groups or individuals. Similarly, many schools will have integration assistants, making it possible for inclusive educational practices to be embedded, although this again could be developed further. Other illustrations of one-to-one tuition include peripatetic music teaching, sports coaching, reading recovery tuition, literacy volunteers and language assistants in secondary schools.

Focused intelligence, the ability to acquire and apply knowledge and know-how, in the new source of wealth. Education is the crucial key to future wealth, but it is a key which takes a long time to shape and a long time to turn. The good news is that everyone can be intelligent in some way or can get intelligent. Intelligence has many faces, all of them useful, all of them potential property in the new world of intelligence. We need to have a clear idea of our best intelligences and learn to make the most of them. It should be the first duty of any school to discover one's intelligences and deploy them.

(Charles Handy, *The Empty Raincoat*, 1994, pp. 206–7)

If the ratio of one-to-one teaching is to be considerably increased then adult volunteers and peer tutors will have to be used much more extensively than at present. Teaching associates such as community leaders, resident artists and sports people have been used successfully in schools. Adult volunteers, often parents but sometimes from the business community or retired people, are mainly used in primary schools, but sometimes in an ancillary rather than a learning situation. Much more can be done to target this resource onto the learning needs of individual pupils. Some of these adult volunteers can be used as mentors rather than simply as speakers or an extra pair of hands in the classroom. Schemes to link pupils with people from the world of business are expanding and can offer real benefits in building self confidence and helping to increase their application to study. Another example of this is the Birmingham KWESI scheme in which Afro-Caribbean boys are mentored by successful role models from the community. Other resources are reading or literacy volunteers from local businesses who regularly work with individual children, and firms who are prepared to second their employees for short-term placements. Peer tutoring whereby 'young teachers' assist 'younger learners', particularly in literacy, numeracy and information technology can be a significant resource to any school, primary or secondary. One primary school has a well established 'Young Teachers' Club' in which older siblings are trained to work with younger brothers and sisters developing reading skills. This is a one step on from traditional shared reading methods, as the children meet in a group to share ideas and problems, have a file in which they record their activities and comments and are expected to share time, both in school and at home. Another secondary school has organised sixth-form pupils to work with Year 7 pupils in improving literacy and numeracy skills. The teaching staff themselves need to analyse when and how they can provide increased tuition. This may be through additional extra-curricular activities such as sport, drama, chess, photography and other clubs and societies, or through curriculum extension, with study opportunities provided before and after school or during breaks in the school day, such as homework clubs, extra revision classes and extra after-school tuition.

Bearing in mind that children and young people are only in school some 15 per cent of their time, the development of a home and community curriculum can offer a great deal in terms of increasing the learning power available. We have seen that individual schools can provide extended opportunities, but these can also be provided collectively by an LEA working in partnership with schools and particular agencies. Birmingham, for example, has established a 'Children's University' to help create a positive attitude to learning amongst primary-aged pupils, encompassing particular groups of schools supported by their parents and communities. Pupils attend tutorial bases after school and in the holidays to study particular 'modules' which offer extended opportunities to learn, with greater individual support. Similarly the University of the First Age (for lower secondary school pupils) provides a mixture of holiday learning experiences, supported self-study opportunities and after-school learning experiences, with schools and the community pooling their efforts to give greater individual opportunities to young people.

There is a considerable range of opportunities for schools to provide additional one-to-one learning opportunities, and the number of staff in schools other than teachers continues to grow. These para-professionals, or teaching associates, working in partnership can provide an enormous boost to the learning opportunities of children and young people. However, sometimes it is a question of organising one-to-one *attention* rather than tuition. For example, a staff concerned to reduce disaffection that may lead to exclusion, temporary or permanent, might decide to brainstorm the names of pupils in Years 7 to 9 who are at risk. All these pupils, unbeknown to them, might be allocated a member of staff who would promise to stop them at least twice a week in the corridor or in social areas of the school to engage them in conversation about school or out-of-school interests. This is likely to have the effect of considerably reducing exclusions and turning some pupils into positive achievers. In general, therefore, critical intervention to deliberately seek to increase one-to-one learning opportunities will make it much more likely that the school is successful for everyone.

Critical steps

- audit one-to-one learning opportunities in the school
- target particular pupils in need
- review the distribution of human resources
- introduce/increase peer tutoring
- introduce/increase business and community volunteers as helpers and mentors
- explore further provision of individual coaching through curriculum extension and extra curricular activities

Unlocking the energy: participation in innovation and research

The personal and professional growth of teachers is closely related to pupil growth. One of the most significant critical interventions a school can make is to invest in learning for all staff and deliberately seek out ways to participate in innovation and research. This can be achieved in a number of ways. It may start from including a commitment to research and further learning in the job descriptions of all members of staff. From there, one could ask how each member of staff could give a learning example to the school. Is it through the observation of classroom practice, the production of an interactive display, reporting back on a learning experience at a staff meeting or through further, accredited study? Whatever the route, the expectation would be that each member of staff would set a learning example; indeed, would have an annual learning plan. From this could be developed a more systematic notion of the teacher as researcher. A successful school will always have a planned series of specific reviews which will involve teachers and other staff in critically evaluating current practices.

A secondary school's research and innovation programme for one year

- An examination of continuity and progression in English through a review of work done in Years 6 and 7
- Researching attitudes to teaching and learning in Years 8 and 9 through interviews and pupil questionnaires, in partnership with a local university
- An investigation into the research skills of particular groups of pupils using the Internet and school library
- Teaching boys separately from girls in certain GCSE subjects, in order to ascertain the impact on raising achievement
- Introducing and researching the effectiveness of a mentoring programme for Year 10 pupils

All staff need to be able to collect and analyse data and contribute to the research-based culture of school improvement. In this way, they will not only be able to reflect on their own practice but influence change within the school generally.

Everyone can make a difference to the craft knowledge of the school

A school geared to innovation and research would have somebody designated as being in charge of research, with possibly a link governor. They would co-ordinate classroom and whole-school reviews and be responsible for the publication and dissemination of research findings. The school would set a target of publishing its action research at least once a year. Further, it would organise and co-ordinate an annual learning conference at which other schools and educationalists would be invited to share their findings and where the key issues of school improvement could be debated and analysed.

The accreditation of learning, whether for parents, lunchtime supervisors, classroom assistants, nursery nurses, school secretaries or teaching staff would be a major feature of the school's provision. There are increasing examples of schools becoming recognised training bases for NVQ level qualifications in, for example, childcare and information technology. There are others who are established outreach professional development centres of further and higher education, providing staff with the means to obtain a range of further qualifications.

Crucially, a school of innovation and research would have dynamic partnerships with higher education and the educational research community as a whole. Teachers would undertake further qualifications, with courses provided partly in the school to allow them to improve both their academic attainment and their classroom performance. The school would attract cohorts of teaching practice students who, as well as learning their craft alongside skilled and trained mentors and coaches, would be expected to undertake small-scale research studies concerning the learning needs of individuals or small groups of pupils. They would be expected to present their findings to the school and suggest ways of improving practice. As part of the school–higher education compact, lecturers in teacher training would be expected to lead staff seminars and workshops and plan joint research activities on a longer timescale with the school. Similarly, 'expert' teachers would be expected to participate in elements of teacher training. Just as some hospitals are designated as 'teaching hospitals', so the school would wish to be designated as a 'teaching school', focusing on research and innovation and constantly seeking to be more effective.

Critical steps

- a collective commitment to undertake reviews and publish active research
- all staff to provide learning examples and annual learning plans
- an annual learning conference
- accreditation of learning for everybody
- teaching and research partnerships with higher education

Raising the standard: setting targets to improve pupils' performance

National testing is now established at 7, 11 and 14, which, together with public examinations at 16 and 18, means that a range of performance information is available at school, LEA and national level. Indeed much of this information is now provided annually to schools through their LEAs and through PANDAs (Performance and Assessment) reports from QCA. It is now a requirement for schools to set targets for improvement based on this data at ages 11 and 16, although targets need not always be strictly related to national assessments and examinations. Schools could critically intervene by self-setting targets to take action at various fixed points to raise educational standards, whether for the school as a whole, certain groups within the school or for individual pupils. A school can only be considered effective if it promotes progress for all its pupils beyond what would be expected given individual attainment and development factors, and school effectiveness research shows how important are high expectations in raising standards of achievement. Quite clearly, schools contribute differently to pupil achievement in terms of added value. This can best be illustrated by reference to the measurement of achievement of those schools placed in similar groups. In Birmingham all schools are grouped in 'families' according to background factors known to impact on pupil achievement such as free school meals, pupils with English as an additional language, prior attainment and pupil turnover. This strategy helps to identify those schools that are making a real difference and succeeding against the odds and enables other schools in the family to share their successful experiences and to set appropriate targets to match their success.

The effective use of targets, especially quantitative targets, helps schools to articulate clearly what is expected of each pupil, class or group – or indeed of the school as a whole and this is clearly set out in the DfEE's publication, *From Targets to Action* (1998). Closely related to target setting is the targeting of particular pupils or groups in order to focus action, support and resources. This could apply to attendance and punctuality patterns as well as to behaviour which clearly, if allowed to go unchecked, will fatally undermine achievement.

As a framework for schools setting targets to raise achievement Birmingham LEA has set out a series of guarantees on a whole-school basis which, as well as establishing targets of input and targets of process or experience, have suggested targets of outcome. (See appendices for descriptions of the Early Years, Primary and Secondary Guarantees.) The Primary Guarantee has two targets of outcome related to improvements in literacy and numeracy. Each school is asked to audit at ages 7 and 11 the percentage of:

- apprentice readers
- foundation readers
- advanced readers
- independent readers

and to agree modest and ambitious targets for decreases in the percentage of apprentice readers and increases in the percentage of advanced and independent readers over the year ahead. Similarly, each school audits at 7 and 11 the percentage of:

- apprentice mathematicians
- foundation mathematicians
- advanced mathematicians
- independent mathematicians

and agrees targets for decreases in the percentage of apprentice mathematicians and increases in the percentage of advanced and independent mathematicians.

These targets relate approximately to National Curriculum levels of assessment and to local and national targets at Key Stage 2, and provide a real stimulus to focusing the energies of staff, parents and the community on raising standards in literacy and numeracy.

The Secondary Guarantee provides a similar framework for schools to set targets to improve literacy and numeracy at the end of Year 7 and in all the core subjects at Year 9, as well as GCSE and vocational qualifications at Year 11. Equal importance is also given to setting targets to *decrease* the number of pupils leaving school without any qualifications. The new statutory targets at 16 of five A–C passes, GCSE point scores and the percentage achieving one or more GCSE pass will easily fit into this pattern.

Although annual target setting can be very effective, the analysis of achievement trends is sometimes better seen using three-year rolling averages and then setting targets over a longer period as well. Thus Birmingham schools were asked to set millennium targets with particular reference to those year groups presently in the school who will be undertaking national assessments and examinations in the year 2000. This links the excitement and expectations of the millennium with the expectation of raising achievement.

Table 4.8 Birmingham schools' Millennium targets

Target groups	Year 2000
Reception children entering school September 1997	KS1 SATs
Year 4 pupils (1997)	KS2 SATs
Year 7 pupils (1997)	KS3 SATs
Year 9 pupils (1997)	GCSE or equivalent
Year 11 pupils (1997)	A level or equivalent

Where schools are serious about raising standards of achievement they will not only publish and display their whole-school targets, indicating their commitment to improve on their previous best, they will also have established targets for particular groups of pupils based on a thorough analysis of the performance of boys and girls and different ethnic minority groups. In the core areas in the primary school and in all subjects in the secondary school there will be a rigorous analysis of achievement data and consideration of anomalies, patterns and trends that will inform the setting of new targets.

Of course, a commitment to target setting as a critical intervention is only effective if it leads to specific actions designed to raise pupils' expectations of themselves and a review of teaching and learning strategies. Three examples from Birmingham schools were published in a DfEE/OFSTED publication on *Setting Targets to Raise Standards* (1996). Prince Albert Primary School identified weaknesses in mathematics through internal assessment. The teachers therefore introduced a range of strategies, both to improve resources for maths and to target groups of pupils for intensive support over a six-week period. These strategies have been underpinned by a curriculum-wide change in classroom management, so that teachers give more sustained support to individual pupils. Techniques include concentrated class teaching, personal mentoring and one-to-one support in class. Using both this 'short burst' approach for intensive targeting and general targets across years, with rigorous monitoring, has enabled the school to make a dramatic improvement in achievement. Down the road and not far from Prince Albert, the Grove Primary School has developed an assessment database which is used to identify and provide for different groups of pupils in the core subjects. Teachers log assessment data from the core subjects into the database every term. They then use the information to select teaching groups for different purposes in 'fast track' English and maths groups, and to identify pupils with particular learning difficulties. For example, pupils in Years 5 and 6 operating at National Curriculum Levels 4 and 6 in English are grouped together; while pupils not reaching Levels 1 or 2 are grouped together for intensive support. Teachers then assess regularly to measure progress and redeploy resources accordingly. In Shenley Court Secondary School, following receipt of estimated GCSE grades early in the year, Year 11 tutors and pupils agree and record individual targets for achievement. Each member of staff mentors three pupils from each year group throughout the year, with subject teachers 'on standby' to offer additional support. Targets, which may be reviewed and adjusted throughout the year, are manageable and precise but challenging, and concern particular aspects of learning which, if improved, would lead to higher grades in the GCSE examinations.

The setting of the targets is most effective when individual teachers are fully involved in devising these targets and take responsibility for their achievement, and the pupils are fully aware of what is expected of them. This can only come about when the school has an ongoing commitment to self-review and evaluation and is prepared to debate honestly and openly where and how it can improve on its previous best.

Critical steps

- The school reviews and analyses achievement data and critically examines anomalies, patterns and trends.
- All staff agree whole-school targets to raise achievement and targets for particular groups, as well as targets for individual pupils.
- The school produces an annual action plan to raise achievement, which is

replicated in core areas in the primary school and all subject departments in the secondary school.

- All staff subscribe to targets to raise standards in literacy and numeracy with a commitment to whole-school policies and practices.
- Ongoing monitoring and evaluation strategies are built into this process.

This may be more succinctly expressed as:

Review the data
Apply the targets
Implement the strategies
Systematically monitor progress
Evaluate the outcomes
   the standard

Promoting a positive ethos: building self-esteem

We know that those who are going to do well in life are marked out by their self-esteem, their motivation and their ability to take responsibility for their own learning.
(John MacBeath, quoted in DfEE, *Extending Opportunity*, 1998, p. 8)

In his work *Multiple Intelligences* Howard Gardner defines interpersonal intelligence as the 'capacity to discern and respond appropriately to the moods, temperaments, motivations and desires of other people', and intrapersonal intelligence as 'access to one's own feelings and the ability to discriminate among them and draw upon them to guide behaviour'. He argues that of all the intelligences, these personal intelligences are the most important and that we need to train children in the personal intelligences in school. This is a theme picked up by Daniel Goleman in his book *Emotional Intelligence*, in which he argues that schools should attempt to teach the core competencies or domains of emotional intelligence, which he terms emotional literacy. These core competencies are referred to as:

- knowing one's emotions
- managing emotions
- motivating oneself
- recognising emotions in others
- handling relationships

A school could make a critical intervention around promoting these competencies, with the particular aim of building self-esteem, which, in turn, would improve children's achievement and enhance the school's ability to teach successfully. To do so would mean the adoption of specific strategies, such as circle time in primary schools or positive use of assemblies. At its heart would be a core personal and social education programme which deliberately set out to develop emotional self-awareness, to help the managing of emotions with more positive feelings about self, school and family, to harness emotions productively, to practise empathy and to improve the handling of relationships, including sharing, co-operation, communicating and helpfulness. Such a course of action could not be undertaken lightly and would have a profound effect on the educational community. It would affect relationships, policies and organisational procedures and would test to the limit the integrity of the school's aims, objectives and values.

> Even though a high IQ is no guarantee of prosperity, prestige, or happiness in life, our schools and our culture fixate on academic abilities, ignoring emotional intelligence, a set of traits – some might call it character – that also matters immensely for our personal destiny. Emotional life is a domain that, as surely as math or reading, can be handled with greater or lesser skill, and requires its unique set of competencies . . . emotional aptitude is a meta-ability; determining how well we can use whatever other skills we have.
>
> (Daniel Goleman, *Emotional Intelligence*, 1996, p. 36)

Many a school's PSE programme will have units of work that reflect the familiar cross-curriculum issues and elements of social studies. However, to change significantly the culture of the school will involve teaching and learning strategies that encourage the development of emotional literacy, the full involvement of pupils in the life and work of the school and the exposure of all pupils to curriculum units and experiences that are part of the shared practice and common language of the school. Such core units would include aspects of equal opportunities, personal responsibility, citizenship, and social and cultural education. In particular, when children (and staff) have all gone through the process of exploring human needs, intelligences and feelings in such units, they can feel part of the objective of making their school a place where their needs are met and their aspirations encouraged and supported. Those schools that are seeking to improve or raise standards through deliberately targeting the raising of pupil self-esteem will be looking to provide openings for pupils to gain success, whatever the nature of their dominant intelligence. This will include the proper recognition of a broad spectrum of achievement, giving all pupils the chance to accept responsibility and the support to do it well, and changing the customs and practices of school organisation to encourage sensitivity to the needs and feelings of others and support the aim of self-actualisation for every individual child.

Indeed, as Goleman says, 'It is not enough to teach children about values: they need to practise them, which happens as children build the essential and social skills. In this sense, emotional literacy goes hand in hand with education for character, for moral development and for citizenship' (*Emotional Intelligence*, p. 286). Particular practices would include the fostering of pupil responsibility and leadership. One aspect of this would be the development of a school or pupil council elected from forms or years, with its own chair and secretary working with representatives of the school senior management team. If meetings were organised once a month, for example, agendas could be debated in classes and the minutes of meetings similarly discussed. In some schools every member of the council has a role – taking minutes, collecting letters from the suggestion boxes, writing articles for the newsletter, and so on. A termly newsletter is published on matters arising, which is discussed in each class and copies kept in the main reception area for visitors to read.

Another strategy would be the appointment of key pupils to help in the running and administration of the school. These are often called prefects, but whatever the title schools who take this seriously prepare job descriptions and person specifications and interview for the posts. This is a valuable lesson in itself. Examples of other specialist responsibilities are librarians and members of a 'bully court'. Both of these involve training and accreditation. Using pupils as skilled librarians or mediators in behaviour issues not only builds their self-esteem but promotes a positive ethos throughout the school.

There are a considerable number of other opportunities that primary and secondary schools can take to develop leadership and responsibility. Many schools adopt the policy of using older pupils as buddies or mentors attached to new pupils coming in to Year 3 or Year 7. Some schools have developed 'hospitality teams' to take major responsibility for hosting events in the school, from invitations to car parking, welcoming, seating and catering. Others have major 'community teams' who take a particular interest in community service, for example 'adopting' senior citizens and particularly needy groups. The running of clubs and societies offers other leadership roles and opportunities to develop whole-school events such as a Young Amnesty Club adopting prisoners of conscience and writing birthday and Christmas cards with messages of hope and support. There are other opportunities to build self-esteem and pupil leadership through the extended curriculum, such as Young Enterprise schemes involved in designing, making and marketing a product or homework clubs which are mainly run and administered by the pupils themselves with their own learning assistants.

A school intent on building self-esteem will strive to deliver, formally and informally, a programme of emotional literacy and involve pupils significantly in the life of their schools, including organisational, environmental and curriculum areas. They will also always strive to put pupils at the centre of their learning, to increase motivation and raise standards of achievement, through self-assessment, target setting and action planning to review work done, to assess progress and to develop personal action plans. Pupils are partners in the school improvement process and can do much, if consulted, to develop this. Indeed, all improving schools involve pupils in the decisions that affect them.

Critical steps

- Establish Gardner's work on the seven intelligences in *The Unschooled Mind* and Goleman's work in *Emotional Intelligence* as a common language for all staff.
- Provide training opportunities to undertake these critical processes.
- In the light of the above, review the school's personal and social education programme, which will include a strong element on citizenship.
- Provide leadership opportunities for pupils, with appropriate training if required.
- Consider the involvement of pupils at all levels of organisational, environmental and curriculum change as part of the overall school improvement strategy.

Mapping interventions

We can apply the grammar of school improvement in the form of interventions – great and small – to all aspects of a school's work. Here are ten chapters of school improvement, with two detailed examples showing how this could be mapped out.

Ten chapters of school improvement

- raising achievement
- learning and teaching
- a research community
- developing the home and community curriculum
- use of information technology
- raising self-esteem
- lifelong learning
- staff development
- curriculum specialisms
- developing inclusive practices

**Learning and teaching:
a programme of interventions**

Punctuations
staffroom noticeboard on learning and teaching
staff meetings in different classrooms
learning plans for all with annual targets

Nouns
effective planning
teaching techniques and repertoire
challenge and expectations
a learning and teaching policy

Verbs
observing each other teaching
practising and learning new strategies
planning, preparing and evaluating learning materials together
monitoring and evaluating

Adjectives
good questioning skills
effective use of ability grouping
good classroom organisation of resources and materials

Adverbial clauses
school as a research community, publishing action research
links to professional development and accreditation
partnerships with higher education/offering school as a case study

---

Raising achievement: a programme of interventions

Punctuation
peer tutoring
praise postcards
homework clubs/subject surgeries

Nouns
maximum learning time/extended learning
achievement focus
high expectations for all

Verbs
coaching and mentoring
monitoring pupil performance: race, gender, special needs
providing one-to-one learning opportunities
reviewing teaching and learning styles

Adjectives
pupil self-esteem enhanced

---

parental and community involvement
effective use of assessment techniques
improved learning environment

Adverbial clauses
annual target setting (school and year group)
long-term target setting (school)
target setting for individual pupils

As we have previously remarked, the quality and range of small and large interventions are crucial success factors in improving schools. Whilst 'butterflies' need to be captured, critical interventions have to be carefully planned. Where there is a shared culture of professional development and action research both butterflies and critical interventions will develop through the process of collective review. Where that culture only partly exists, schools may only stumble across interventions and will end up with a very ad hoc approach to improvement. Interventions need to be systematically mapped, planned, implemented, and evaluated as the prime means of improving schools against their previous best.

The road to school improvement is always under construction.

In which the CEO loses a letter, makes a rash promise, discovers a jewel and celebrates the achievements of the energy creators

Most Brummies have heard of Heybarnes. Anybody giving directions to a driver lost in that part of the city will refer to Heybarnes and the Asda stores as landmarks close to Small Heath which punctuate the route from the Coventry Road or Small Heath Highway towards the International Airport and the National Exhibition Centre.

I bet you didn't know that 300 yards away from Heybarnes under the chimney of the Tyseley Waste Disposal Unit and in the grounds of T I Reynolds is a jewel. Hay Hall has fifteenth-century features with beautifully warm Tudor and other later additions.

Ten years ago Hay Hall was restored to its former glory by T I Reynolds with grants from the city council, on the condition that it would be used for educational purposes. Recently the Central Area 4 (CA4) consortium of schools had a celebration there. It was most impressive, complementing in the sparkling kaleidoscope of teaching and learning the surroundings of Hay Hall. There were confident performances of drama, dance, song and poetry from 10- and 11-year-old youngsters from a sample of CA4 schools. The rooms of Hay Hall displayed each school's presentation of their particular part of the jigsaw of CA4, the whole creating a map of the area built on the 84 features or sites of environmental interest they had identified.

It all started from a mistake on my part. Let me explain.

A year or so ago I received a begging letter from a 'consortium of schools' called CA4, which, as you will have gathered, hails from that part of the city. The letter's message, put simply, was that if progress was to be made on both the environmental and residential experience included in the Primary Guarantee, it would be made best if the schools in an area worked together rather than separately. CA4, the letter suggested, got together mainly to share information at headteacher level. 'But we could share resources and plan together to carry out the environmental experience. It could give us some purpose . . . so could we have £5,000?' I then mislaid the letter for some months – nothing unusual in that, do I hear you think?

When I replied, in a surge of guilt I compounded my incompetence by confessing that I had no idea where to get the money from but the temptation to encourage co-operation among schools was so great that I'd find the £5,000 from somewhere, on the condition that the schools would find more than a matching amount from their own resources. I then added, cheekily, that I wondered where CA4 was in the city, confessing to my newcomer's ignorance but going on to say ironically 'In style of identity, CA4 certainly has a ring to it – a bit like School number 1287, New York East Central District.'

Less than a year later at the celebratory events CA4 revealed to me and many other admirers not just the jewel of Hay Hall but also the full panoply of their creative work together.

It wasn't simply the written work, the performances, the tourist map. It was much more. Symbolic of the much more was the Pledge Tree creative statue, an icon, as the name implies, in a representation of a tree, to which were attached various pledges from Year 5 and Year 6 pupils in CA4 schools. These young people were committing themselves, not just in principle but through weekly talks, to maintain, cherish and develop the environment, not only in their own schools but including pillar boxes, telephone kiosks, mosques, temples, churches, roads, homes and the open space of their various immediate neighbourhoods. Moreover, they could see how the various pieces of the jigsaw of CA4 made up the whole district community depending for its strength on the sum of the parts. So industrial sites, transportation routes and methods, commerce, housing, schools, places of worship and nature itself, whether red in tooth and claw or farmed in parks and other recreational places, were together their own past, present and future. Above all, the Pledge Tree gave both a sense of their understanding that the community was theirs to shape for the twenty-first century and that they were determined to make it better.

It was probably romantic of me to think that I was present at the beginning of a new 'rite' which a hundred years on would still be celebrated by young successors in Cole Heath (for that's how CA4 has renamed itself). It is probably too fanciful to speculate that future historians will see the last years of this century as a time when we reasserted our belief in society as something more than the pursuit of the individual and self-gratification – and in our individual self-fulfilment as depending on our interdependence and on wanting as much for other people's children as we want for our own.

As somebody once said 'Our future depends on that – on the work of educators.' CA4 – sorry, Cole Heath – reminded me of that and of how fortunate we are in Birmingham to have so many 'energy creators'. These are that group of staff for whom every cup is more than half full,

143

who start every sentence with 'That's a good idea' or 'What if' or 'Let's try' and who are full of infectious enthusiasm and generosity. They affect those of us in the second group who do our job because it's there – and privately we know it's the most important job. We take pride in our work and from time to time we get inspired to achieve amazing feats which surprise and delight not merely ourselves but others. Thankfully in Birmingham there are so few of a third group, the energy consumers, for whom every silver lining has 25 or so clouds and who are always reminding us why something can't be done.

So I'm glad I lost that letter from the Cole Heath consortium and then, guilt ridden, made a rash promise. Hay Hall is for anyone to use for a conference or a celebration of the arts or for music, and at no cost. Just ring the headteacher of Hobmoor Primary School, although I suspect Cole Heath has plenty of plans to work together, not least to renew the Pledge Tree. Of course, the whole jigsaw of the city could be complete if other consortia took similar action. But please don't write. It's too costly if I lose the letter.

5

STAKEHOLDERS AND PARTNERS

Their contribution to school improvement

Any school operates within a local and national context and is as affected by
the climate set by the media and the institutional partners with whom they
relate – principally central government and local government, the teachers'
associations and other unions – as it is by the behaviour and attitude of its own
individual stakeholders. A wet dinner time, for example, is a challenging
local and immediate climate for a school: it will immediately affect and test the
school's capacity to sustain a purposeful and fulfilling atmosphere amongst
pupils and staff alike. In a similar way, the school's life is affected by the
announcements of the Secretary of State when he or she issues guidelines on
homework. The media's reaction to that – articles by Melanie Phillips, Michael
Barber, Ted Wragg's column, the articles and utterances of Chris Woodhead
and the teacher associations' leaders – all combine at the immediate crises of
the moment, and over a period on other policy matters, to create a kind of educational weather. This affects the attitudes brought initially to a school by all
stakeholders, which will be more or less positive or negative in consequence of
what happens as a result of the national weather forecast.

The LEA, we believe, has the duty and capacity to affect that climate by the
way it behaves towards its schools. It has to choose where to strike the balance
between challenge, pressure and support. Each LEA has a different historical
inheritance. In *what* the LEA does and *how* it does it, the LEA will perpetuate
or change the climate it has created locally. That local climate can powerfully
moderate the national climate created by legislation, the actions and voice of
the DfEE (ministers and officials), the various quangos, OFSTED and by the
media. Some believe that the national climate, which was one of benign
neglect for many years until the late 1980s, has turned into what is best
likened to a hailstorm of externally imposed change.

This book is punctuated by 'interludes'. They are all accounts drawn from
Birmingham's *Education Bulletin*, a journal which is published five or six
times a year. It contains news, lists events and there are always a few articles.
The 'Tim Talking' series of articles started when the officer responsible for
the *Bulletin* asked for an article from the newly appointed CEO by way of an
introduction to the whole service. Soon he was asked to contribute a second,

and then a third, and so it has become a chance to write repeatedly about particular issues with a common theme in the knowledge that the *Bulletin* will lie on staffroom tables and be read by a few and talked about by others. It is a chance to affect climate. So too are appearances by local politicians, officers, advisers, governors and parents on local newspaper and radio stations.

But writing articles in bulletins and appearing with consistent messages on radio stations and on the television screen is nothing if the prevailing climate is not one of celebrating success, or if the regular transactional purposes of the LEA are conduced in a bureaucratic manner. So circulars need to be colour-coded and each missive needs to make explicit, with a clear summary, whether it is legislatively required or advisory, whether there is a cost involved and whether it is information that a head or governors can usefully put on one side for future reference or something that requires urgent action. Similarly, hand-written appreciation notes sent to teachers and support staff across a very large schooling system will probably not appear systematic, even when they are, and if they can occasionally reinforce the worth of people, for example, advisers, educational social workers or psychologists who have commented positively on the work of colleagues in schools, then the whole climate turns into one of 'appreciative enquiry'.

'Appreciative enquiry' is a form of management first articulated in a theoretical form in an article about the work of Cooperrider and Srivasta. They compared 'appreciative enquiry' with 'problem solving' as two possible forms of management. Of course the latter is more familiar, involving a four-stage process as set out below:

Problem Solving
1   Identify a problem or a felt need.
2   Analyse the causes.
3   Brainstorm the solutions.
4   Decide on a plan of action.

It seems to us that this model of management is necessarily prevalent in a world of accountability and regulation, where there is frequent inspection and a propensity among those who inspect to identify weaknesses and difficulties. All these, of course, have to be addressed and the four steps of 'problem solving' outline in simple form what is essentially a method of avoiding complacency and building on collective review (see chapter 2). It is a simple, if unremarkable and obvious way of proceeding. Most readers will be familiar with the sequence.

Less well understood, however, is Cooperrider and Srivasta's model of 'appreciative enquiry'. This may be represented simply as follows:

Appreciative enquiry
1   Appreciate the best of *what is*.
2   Ask *what it could be like* if you could only have more of the good things identified.
3   Discourse in order to find out *what it should be like*.
4   Decide *what it will be like*.

This model has particular attractions for us since it builds on existing strengths, whereas an over-reliance on problem solving might be seen as a deficit model and one, therefore, which saps energy rather than creates it. Typically, elements of 'appreciative enquiry' would be manifest in heads of department, subject co-ordinators and headteachers who frequently exclaim on and celebrate good practice, drawing it to the attention of the wider community and thus encouraging speculation about emulating what has been identified. Again, it is a model that can be seen to align simply with the practices of collective review, but with the difference that it is less threatening and there is less danger of the loss of energy which, as we have remarked, is such a vital – if elusive – commodity in school life.

Our point in setting out these two models is to illustrate how climates can be set by managerial styles and by the choice of emphasis within an institution, or by those who affect an institution. Indeed, the climate within a school is often affected, as we have argued, by the institutional stakeholders. We set out earlier ways in which a local education authority, for example, can, for better or worse, affect the likelihood of the internal climate-setting mechanisms of a school being inclined towards the positive or the negative.

Of course there is a third model not found in the literature. We think it is equally valid as a management model, and one which is different from either problem solving or climate setting. We would term that third model 'ensuring compliance'. The equivalent four processes are set out as follows:

Ensuring compliance
1   Decide what is right.
2   Regulate that the single solution will be implemented by everyone.
3   Inspect to ensure that the solution is being followed.
4   Publicly punish deviants and inadequates.

We believe that there is a danger that such a model will be the unintentional result of some national actions. This is clearly more likely to happen when, as is now the case, we have Secretaries of State who can exercise an enormous number of powers rather than at a time when the Secretary of State had only three powers to affect the system, as was the case some years ago.

The danger, of course, with this model, even without its fourth step, is that should it be accompanied, as it is, with a thorough model of external inspection, the likelihood is that schools will find their lives dominated by a dangerous combination of 'ensuring compliance' and 'problem solving'. It is in our view, all the more important that the less remarked model of 'appreciative enquiry' is given attention by those who affect the school on a daily basis.

The need for a 'critical friend'

That brings us to the question of a school's need for a 'critical friend'. When we initially discussed the idea, we knew that we were being heavily influenced, as we were in a number of our 'theory-influenced' actions in school improvement, by Michael Fullan. His elaboration of the ideas of 'critical friends', and the 'friendly critics' or 'uncritical friends' attracted us. We would recast them as:

- the *'hostile witness'*: someone who so disapproves of the activity of the school that they bring to their involvement in the life of the school a bias towards negativity that is at once condemnatory
- the *'uncritical lover'*: someone who is so besotted with what they perceive as the all-embracing success of the school that they could tend to devalue the currency of praise because all their comments are undifferentiately positive.
- the *'critical friend'*: someone who understands and is sympathetic to the purpose of the school, knows its circumstances very well, is skilled in offering a second opinion, or sometimes a first opinion, about an issue only half perceived by the school itself, or if perceived, seen as impenetrable.

We set out in what follows the characteristics of hostile witnesses, uncritical lovers and critical friends.

Hostile witnesses:
- use 'you' a lot
- tend to tell and judge rather than listen and ask open questions
- bring preferred and singular views of schools and teaching and learning practice which they overlay on their schools
- write, as a matter of course, judgemental notes on schools and teachers which they do not share with the teachers/schools
- have ready-made answers to a school's problems
- do not discuss evidence for judgements
- are strong on assertion and opinion
- do not become involved (except judgementally) at times of school crisis

Uncritical lovers:
- do not write notes on school visits or teacher exchanges
- identify 'good' practice individually (and have no shared yardstick for its value)

148

- overdo praise, scattering it indiscriminately and thereby reducing its value
- only ask rhetorical questions to affirm the school's/teacher's position
- spend time at ceremonial events, but rarely go beyond the head's room or assembly-type events
- tend to use time only once
- forget to follow up on promised action
- do not mention articles or papers they have read

Critical friends:
- are immediately accessible at times of school crisis
- ask questions which increasingly focused, but speculative not judgemental
- use 'we' and 'you' (but not 'I' except to promise or take blame) in equal measure
- when giving a view leave sentences or questions half-finished to preserve dignity
- identify personally and equally with a school's successes and its failures
- enable the school to carry out internal self-evaluation and ask after the process, often identifying external witnesses
- see strengths as well as points for development
- balance 'appreciative enquiry' with 'problem solving'
- anticipate schools' sensitive occasions

It will be seen that critical friends, like good teachers and good heads of department or phase heads, are seemingly effortlessly skilled at asking questions. They bring to that questioning task a mastery of inflection and timing, so that questions are never damaging. They speculate aloud so that the development of their thinking is shared, as though with a third party, when they sift the evidence of a possible line of enquiry. When hard messages are necessary, they are often conveyed in the form of half-finished questions. If presented in the form of statements, the liberal use of the first or the third person, rarely the second person, punctuates their remarks.

Critical friends are invaluable to schools. Almost all the case studies in the research (Maden and Hillman's *Success against the odds*, for example) refer to people who, if not described precisely as critical friends, are clearly in that role. References in the case studies to the helpful LEA impact of consultancy refer to either a curriculum or a whole-school adviser who has visited the school and contributed to its renewed sense of direction or purpose. What they never imply is complete satisfaction with all external contacts. We do believe, however, that people external to the school should examine the three possible interpretations of their actions set out in this section. They will then have a better chance of adjusting their contact styles with different schools in order to meet their different needs, with the common purpose of appearing as a critical friends rather than the alternatives of uncritical lovers or hostile witnesses.

A school needs a range of critical friends for different aspects of school life.

Every school, even Eton and Harrow, needs a critical friend, or rather a series of critical friends. Each critical friend needs a precise and focused specialism, but also some wider peripheral vision in order to be sure that they are building levels of energy (perhaps through appreciative enquiry). In such a way they look at English, music, art, indeed the whole curricular range of academic subjects. Somebody with a broader brief will look at the school as a whole – its management and its daily life in corridors, staffrooms, staff meetings, in playgrounds, governors' meetings, after-school clubs and societies, as well as its relationships with a wider local community. They will observe attendance patterns of staff and pupils alike, as well as those who arrive early and leave late. There are, of course, internal members of a school community who will bring to discussions the invaluable trait of open-ended questioning. Colleagues can act as evidence collectors so that together they monitor and evaluate the evidence collected, the better to inform their actions in what will be slightly adjusted new directions. These activities are all part of collective review and show the process characteristics of critical friendship, even if they are essentially derived from stakeholders who are insiders too. Practices such as work-shadowing between schools – for example, a teacher work-shadowing and observing another teacher or a head doing the same thing – can develop the opportunity for critical friendship, even if the main purpose in the short term and the original design was to extend knowledge or some aspect of skill or process being practised by another in similar circumstances.

This brings us to the issue of stakeholders.

The main stakeholders in a school – if we define a stakeholder as someone having a stake in the school's success – are of course those who live and work in the school itself. So the pupils have a principal claim to attention. Indeed, the literature of school improvement and effectiveness is replete with encouragement to involve pupils in decisions about their work and the running of the school.

One of the climate-setting articles within our education bulletin describes briefly the practice of a junior school teacher whose school policy involves all the pupils in applying for classroom jobs. The school has a rigorous principle of pupils taking on leadership and management tasks in their 'houses' as well as in their own class and the school as a whole. Secondary schools which have marking policies involving students themselves assessing their own work, to which the teacher responds, are also involving the stakeholder pupils. So too are primary schools which encourage peer mediation and circle time.

Stakeholders, as we have seen, may be described as those who have a stake in a school's success. They often work in partnership with other stakeholders, either as individuals or institutions who combine to improve the likelihood of their success. There are major and minor stakeholders and partners.

Major stakeholders and partners are those who have the most to gain or lose by a particular school's performance. If looked at in that way, it becomes clearer why central government is prepared to adopt a name and blame approach in which those most closely involved in a school will be revolted by its failings.

The nearer the individual or institution is to a school, the greater the stake-holding.

If that principle is accepted, it becomes possible to draw up a pecking order of stakeholders, as follows:

1 pupils
2 parents
3 support staff
4 headteacher
5 teaching staff
6 governors
7 neighbours of the school
8 local MPs and councillors
9 LEA
10 ministers
11 government

These classifications are mainly composed of individuals and we have considered most of their interests either directly or indirectly during the course of this book. We have placed support staff ahead of teaching staff because in most areas of the country the support staff are more likely to live and work in the vicinity of the school and have their children attend the school. We accept that is not invariably the case; we are just making the point that the investment of some-one working in the school and living close by – certainly if they are a parent too – is greater than that of someone living in a different community altogether.

What the support staff say in their local community affects the school's reputation.

Moreover, the wise school realises that the most powerful messages from adults about a school get carried through the local community by those who work there. So its midday supervisors, the school's secretary, the learning assistant and the meals staff are more likely to carry the reputation of the school than heads of department. This of course has all sorts of implications for staff development as a key process and provisions that are made for support staff in the school more widely.

According to the school's context, stakeholders bring more or less capacity to their task. So Eton and other privately endowed schools have more resources with which to buy more staff and resources. Even history is on their side. More likely than not, all the parents of children at such schools want them to succeed. Even within the state maintained sector, however, there are savage inequalities in a system that ranges from the affluent single-community school where primary school children are dropped off and collected by au pairs at one extreme, through to drab, grey, dilapidated buildings occupied by children from surrounding run-down, half-abandoned estates on the other. In those communities, huge securities set the scene and parents have sometimes given up the unequal struggle of getting themselves or their children to school. Then, of course, there are the schools – the majority of our schools – that lie somewhere in between.

The nearer a school is to poverty, the less likely it is that the children's backgrounds will have that sense of consistent support that gives any child and the school they attend such a head start in unlocking talent and potential. It is as though the stakeholders in such a situation are more loosely and less permanently coupled to the school's purpose: indeed, in such situations turbulence and mobility of pupils is a daily reality. Moreover, in such situations, schools require energy, drive, skill and enthusiasm to a disproportionate degree as they sustain an unrelenting press for pupil achievement. In short, the poorer the context, the more prevalent high unemployment and high crime levels locally, the more important it is for the local school to have as few weak links as possible amongst staff. Sickness amongst staff in such situations can be a severe blow. High turnover rates amongst staff and pupils make sustaining any semblance of school progress a seemingly intractable exercise.

Governors

The relationship of the governing body and a whole-school, through individual members, with the head, other staff and other parents is the most unresearched part of school effectiveness and improvement. Governors have been given a much more powerful position of influence in the school system since the mid-1980s. They have many powers which were formerly exercised by the LEA, indeed, in the grant maintained sector they now replace LEA functions even more substantially.

In our experience, at any one time there will be one or two per cent of school governing bodies which are at loggerheads with the head and/or some other part of the school's management. Certainly, headteachers who are losing their grip will either seek to magnify the governing body (in order to bolster their position) or seek to keep the governing body in the dark (in order to 'keep the lid' on the situation). The position of staff governors when things go wrong is extremely difficult.

As we have said, though, such cases amount to no more than one or two per cent. In the main, the relationship between the head and the governors is not problematic: perhaps the key in this is to help and encourage governors when things are going well so that their work in its own right can sustain improvement.

Unlike other stakeholders, governors represent not only themselves but also a constituent group such as parents, staff, the LEA or the community. They particularly need to work hard at being the 'critical friend' to the head and the staff: this requires them to be known in the school, otherwise their questions will be seen as hostile or irrelevant.

Governing bodies now have four main tasks:

- to provide a strategic view of where the school is heading and help to decide the school's strategy for improvement so that its pupils learn most effectively and achieve the highest standards
- to monitor and evaluate educational standards and the quality of education provided, asking challenging questions and pressing for improvement
- to assume direct responsibility for oversight of financial management, the recruitment of senior staff and some disciplinary matters
- to act as critical friend to a school, providing the headteacher and staff with support, advice and information, drawing on members' knowledge and experience

In carrying out these targets there needs to be a clear understanding by governors and heads of the difference between management and governance. In practice, most governing bodies work through a series of processes and find themselves to a greater or lesser extent 'advising', 'steering', 'mediating', 'supporting' and 'holding the school to account'. Whilst each governing body will decide for itself *how* it should be involved in the running of a school, like all other partners it should demonstrate a commitment to continuous improvement, both in terms of improving the quality of education for the pupils and also in developing its own learning capacity and that of most of the whole-school community. This will mean the setting of a climate in which there is open discussion among governors, the head, staff, parents and sometimes pupils to ensure that there is a shared, common language about roles and responsibilities. As so often in school improvement, the process is the key. Governors also have a vital role in policymaking, development planning and monitoring and evaluation, and will wish to be informed and inform themselves about a school's strengths and weaknesses so that they can work effectively with the head and staff in particular.

A strong school will be made up of various elements of which the governing body is a vital backbone and backstop.
(Sylvia West, *Education Values for School Leadership*, 1993, p. 88)

There are a number of ways in which governors can make a significant contribution to school improvement. The following are a number of suggestions which pick up on the grammar of interventions and processes.

Governors and development planning

Governors can participate fully in development planning if a development planning day for all governors is set aside each year, well in advance. On a development planning day governors work alongside staff in conducting an audit and setting targets (both general and for pupil attainment) for next year's school development plan. The subsequent monitoring of the plan can be helped by giving each sub-committee responsibility for reporting on a key element of the plan. A similar process is necessary when discussing the post-OFSTED inspection plan and integrating this into the school development plan as a whole. The more governors, like staff, can be involved in planning together, the larger the outcome.

Progress reports from departments/phases

The schedule for governing body meetings needs a rolling programme of progress reports. These can cover the work of individual subject departments in the secondary school and particular curriculum areas in the primary school, ideally including both quantifiable and quantitative data. It is also useful to discuss the structure of the termly headteacher's report with the head, so that it enables regular review by all the governing body.

Assigned governors

In some places specific governors are successfully linked to phase/aspect or curriculum leaders in primary and special schools and to heads of department in secondary schools. These governors 'champion' these particular areas and take a direct interest in pedagogy, resources and achievement. They are well placed to help prepare and receive reports to the governing body. Already a 'responsible' governor has a statutory role related to special educational needs in the school, working closely with the special educational needs co-ordinator (SENCO), but this concept could be widened considerably. Other examples would be a governor given prime responsibility for equal opportunities issues or, similarly, health and safety. Whatever the link role, it is important to draw up a short job description so that everybody is clear about their role.

Governor visits

It is true to say that governors who do not visit the school during the working day will always struggle to have credibility in the school community. Visits, moreover, give governors the chance to evaluate the impact of their plans and policies on the day-to-day operation of the school. However, it is important to have a visiting policy, with a code of practice negotiated with the staff, which lays down the different of circumstances and occasions for visits and criteria for whether there are to be written outcomes reported back to the governing body. Misunderstanding about the purpose of visits is widespread in our experience, especially when they are in the planning stage.

Workshops with parents

Curriculum workshops for parents and the community can provide an opportunity for practical examples of learning which help the dignity of staff. In a primary school that takes governors and parents seriously, the 'literacy' and 'numeracy' hours will provide a great opportunity for workshops which draw the community together within learning. Information and communications technology workshops in any phase are another excellent way of developing a shared understanding, whilst enlarging personal capacity. To the delivering school these are also a chance to tap the expertise of governors and parents. There is also a particular role for 'link' governors in taking responsibility for particular areas.

Rotation of governor meetings

When governing body meetings are held in different classrooms or areas of the school, and when each meeting begins with a short presentation from the 'host' staff about specific curriculum, teaching and learning issues, the focus of the governors' discussion is being set. For example, a governing body which meets in the nursery/reception area in one of our schools has a way of engaging in debate about the quality of provision in the early years, baseline assessment, links with parents and other related issues. Similarly, a governing body which meets in the arts faculty of a secondary school and as part of its agenda considers more fully the resourcing and provisions of the arts curriculum will persuade the arts faculty that they are taking their concerns seriously. Such meetings can only be 'tasters' before other governing body business but they add considerably to the knowledge and capacity of governing bodies to make key decisions and, if the host staff stay as observers, facilitate good and informed relations between staff and governors.

Governors' communications

Governors need to be 'visible', in the sense that if they are to be the body which is accountable for the school the pupils, the parents, the staff and a wider community need to know of their work and their role. All the usual media will need to be considered to ensure that this happens. These will include newsletters, displaying photographs of the governors in school along with the rest of the staff, regular open sessions or 'surgeries' and participation in school events. In particular, the best governing bodies think imaginatively about how best to use the legal requirement for governing bodies to hold an annual meeting for parents. This can be one of the high points of a school's calendar but sadly it is often written off as a chore and poorly attended. The best governing bodies see it as a real opportunity for governors, head and staff to present their report to parents and seek advice and help on further improvements. Some governing bodies have taken full advantage of this opportunity by including pupil references, using 'witness stands' and video records of the school's work and achievements. Some combine it with a school performance.

Working on specific sub-committees or joint task groups with other partners in the school provides another opportunity for governors to be more widely known. Sub-committees such as finance and resources, premises, personnel and curriculum can help concentrate expertise to the benefit of the school, but specific task groups can also be useful in building effective partnerships with teaching staff, parents and the local community in the production of joint reports to all governors.

Governors' induction and training

Those schools which take governors seriously allocate mentors and provide induction packs and briefings. New and existing governors need key documentation such as existing policies and plans, reports on the school, pupil performance data and basic administration information. Mentors are usually other governors but having additional mentoring from a member of staff is also very beneficial.

Training and accrediting learning for governors are most often arranged through specifically designed programmes, usually from the Governor Training Unit of an LEA, but sometimes through higher education. Governors are entitled to access to training and, like all learners, need to be encouraged and valued, so why not certificate specific training experience, either in the school or at a local centre? Training in topics such as understanding school performance data and target setting, monitoring and evaluation, financial management, and personnel issues are the logical next step in developing the governor's role in improving schools. Moreover, the change in standards funding which specifies a percentage of the budget for governor training will facilitate this.

Celebrating success

Celebrating success can be overlooked unless it is carefully planned in the routine of the school. This may consist of the involvement of a rota of governors in the weekly awards assembly or participation in enriched extra-curricular activities such as the performing arts, sport, clubs and societies, residential experiences or celebrating a successful OFSTED report. Certainly, all governors need to be involved in some of the range of experiences and activities provided by the school so that they can feel that they are part of a celebrating community as well as an improving community of learners. They may often be used to present certificates and commendations, but it is important that governors themselves are valued for their contribution, through the imaginative use of awards for significant service.

Good partnerships with governors are essential if school improvement is to be sustained. Governing bodies have a vital role in establishing a collaborative culture that encompasses staff, pupils, parents and the wider community. Governors can make schools better by shaping and guarding the values and vision of the school through its key roles of strategic planning and monitoring and evaluation.

> The key characteristic of the effective governing body is its ability to understand and implement the *distinctive* contribution it can make to the management of the school.
>
> (Nigel Gann, *Improving School Governance*, 1998)

We have tried in this chapter to reflect on the importance of climate-setting and the school's need for critical friends. The contribution of stakeholders and partners to school improvement is best done through appreciative enquiry, building on existing strengths through a process of collective review. As critical friends LEAs, parents, governors and other partners are invaluable to schools, in that they ask focused questions such as 'How well are we doing?' 'How do we compare with similar schools?' 'What more should we achieve?' 'What must we do to make it happen?' Stakeholders and partners need to strike a careful balance between pressure and support. If they can do this, working with each other, there will be an increased likelihood of success.

'So what', she asked, 'Is your number one priority?'

The person sitting opposite was a new primary adviser due to take up her post in September. 'So what', she asked as she was winding down the hour-long conversation about the difference between teaching, head-ship and being an adviser, 'is your number one priority?' And seeing the look of thoughtful doubt bordering on panic in my eyes, she decided to fill the silence to give me more time to think. 'You see, I would like to know that at the back of my mind I can take any chance that presents itself to press the issues you think most important in transforming educational standards in the city.'

'Only one?' I muttered, still playing for time, but knowing that she was right to avoid such a plethora of priorities that nobody takes any of them at all seriously. (She had, after all, been a successful headteacher who knew the importance of focusing and insisting on a few important shared objectives.) 'Well, I reckon it would be to multiply fourfold the average vocabulary of the 7-year-olds, 9-year-olds and ll-year-olds in the city. If we could do that we would have cracked it.'

That led us into a long conversation embracing speaking, listening, reading and writing vocabularies, with an important excursion too into the often overlooked importance of ensuring that bilingual children develop the language of the home very strongly, so that the 'transference of a lan-guage scaffolding, into English will as it were, be easier since it will build on a confident grasp of the first language. We talked too of the technique used in successful schools which have analysed the vocabulary of Reception, Year 1 children and so on, up the school. Using that analysis they have then taken a whole-school and staff decision to extend the vocabulary of every child in every year group, both in spoken and written form, and shared the vocabulary with the parents. So the vocabulary extension informs the conversation of staff meetings and of their own reviews of individual children's progress, as well as classroom displays and assemblies. We agreed that in the best schools the extension of vocabulary is not just planned collectively, but monitored collectively too. It is as much a part of topic and theme work as it is of subject and con-versation.

We agreed – this 'shortly to be ex-headteacher and soon to be adviser' and I – that one of the features of the curriculum tests in maths and sci-ence for ll-year-olds was the barrier some children faced as a result of impoverishment or misunderstanding of language. That, of course, is why secondary schools are so anxious to extend the vocabulary of Year 7 children so they can cope with the language demands of the secondary curriculum. As secondary teachers we are more challenged to keep up a 'shared language' set of practices because, of course, we tend to be specialists in one subject and have not been formally trained in the teaching of English 'across the curriculum'. Not for us that essential burning interest in language, numeracy and some aspects of the arts which is the distinguishing feature of all successful primary colleagues.

I once came across a secondary school which took the challenge of language across the curriculum seriously by means of a clever device in Years 7 and 8. Among many other things they adopted a simple scheme, mentioned in the Birmingham book *School Improvement Butterflies* (ed. D C Woods, 1997). It involved the staff of each faculty in turn nominating on a Friday morning five words with definitions which every teacher, from whatever subject area, would use and define at least once in their teaching in each Years 7 and Year 8 class the following week. Each promised to throw in another word to confuse Year 7 and 8, who were enlisted in a competition to spot the five common words. The first out of the draw earned a prize – a year's subscription to a magazine of their choice. Almost as crazy as the teacher who kept a red book which she ostentatiously filled in from time to time when teaching a class. 'I collect things,' she explained defiantly to the inevitable enquiring pupils and kept her secret, increasing the suspense. In the end she admitted that she had collected words and shared their various usages with the children.

Earlier than that – indeed from the cradle – vocabulary extension is crucial, especially since we know how effortlessly the young child can learn. A headteacher working closely with a doctor shared with me the Wellstar research in Manchester. Apparently, the health visitors there use a simple schedule to check, at between 11 and 14 months, those babies who are experiencing language development difficulty either receptively, or expressively, or in terms of behavioural distraction. Then a group of locally employed language workers trained by the speech therapy service, help the parents and wider community to practice various interventions with the babies. As you will have already guessed, the outcome, traced every five years, is extremely positive. We are talking to the health service about it already to see if we can do something similar in Birmingham.

Back to my 'shortly to become an adviser'. One of the features of successful advisers is being able to ask the right questions in the right manner at the right time. David Woods, our chief adviser, often reminds me and his colleagues of the need for those who act as coaches to schools and teachers to find that finely judged lodging place of being the 'critical friend', avoiding the Scylla of the 'unloving critic' – which seems to me the particular hazard of OFSTED, though many of their teams splendidly avoid it – and the Charybdis of the 'uncritical lover'. If one were to caricature, the 'unloving critic' asks too few questions and makes too many judgements, while the 'uncritical lover' makes none and simply echoes in an unfocused way the view we have of ourselves. Every school needs a 'critical friend'. The school needs to know that the 'critical friend' has an empathy with and understanding of its task, their challenges, its success and its setbacks. If the 'critical friend' then has insight, good powers of observation and deduction, she can ask the pointed question that enables the school or the teacher to learn and move on. Above all, she must leave the school and the member of staff with more energy to move the issue forward.

I thought I would get my own back on the 'shortly to become adviser'. So I said that when she had been in post a year I would ask her the following questions.

Questions for advisers

- When did the teachers in the schools for which I'm responsible last have a chance to visit and observe a teacher in comparable circumstances? When is the next occasion scheduled?
- What criteria do these teachers use for the observations?
- What is the declared policy and practice of learning and teaching in the schools for which I'm responsible?
- What focused practice is designed to boost the achievement and attainment of children of Pakistani, Bangladeshi and Afro-Caribbean origins?
- What are the actions I take that genuinely boost the self-esteem of teachers and other staff in the schools that I visit?
- What are the questions I ask which stretch the school or the staff to improve their practice?
- How do my actions in the school take on the development points arising from OFSTED?
- Do I know what progress 'my' schools are making in each of the seen processes of school improvement? Are they improving, staying the

same or even getting worse? Have I shared that perception with the head and chair of governors?

- Which of my schools is improving in terms of achievement and attainment fastest?
- Which is the best 'matching' school in terms of ethnicity, and socio-economic circumstances and what are its comparable results? Has my school visited them? What does my colleague adviser think are the most interesting and promising aspects (i.e. the things that are making a difference) of that school's work?
- What questions do I use that encourage the collection of evidence and cause schools to speculate about the evaluations?
- For my subject phase, which is the most successful practice in the city? How does the practice I am visiting relate to it? What actions would enable the practice to improve?

Appendix 1

SCHOOL IMPROVEMENT

The Birmingham perspective

ESTABLISHING A COMMON LANGUAGE Principles, Processes and Purposes (Leadership, Management and Organisation, Creating an Environment, Teaching and Learning, Staff Development, Collective Review, Parental Involvement)	CREATING THE CLIMATE (Education Department Development Strategy and Initiatives; Guarantees of inputs, processes and targets of outcome, 'Years of . . .', University of the First Age, Children's University, Success for Everyone)

Effective Classrooms/Schools

MONITORING AND MEASURING ACHIEVEMENT (Baseline Assessment, target setting, value added programmes, benchmarking and family groups, monitoring standards over time, analysing achievement by race, gender and special educational needs)	NETWORKING SCHOOLS AND STAFF (Professional development and management programmes, 'Butterflies', Quality Development, Partnerships, Consortia, Databases of good practice, curriculum conferencing)

IMPROVING ON PREVIOUS BEST

Appendix 2

THE EARLY YEARS GUARANTEE (OUTLINE)

TARGETS OF INPUT

- A % increase in the budget for the pre-five education provision over a period of five years.
- An interdepartmental approach to the provision of quality services within the early years.
- Access to international and local networks and expertise to accelerate improvements in the education and care of the under-fives.

Targets of process or experience

- Parents are their child's first educators – materials are produced which provide parents/carers with many ideas for supporting their child's learning in the early years.
- The magic of stories, jingles and rhymes – 1000 stories to be heard or read together; 100 musical tunes and jingles to be sung; 10 nursery rhymes to be shared and memorised.
- Leading to Reading Projects – All children under five to have an opportunity to participate in a 'Leading to Reading' project.
- Caring and Sharing – Every under-five child to have an opportunity of undertaking a visit and/or an environmental project.
- Expressing and Showing – Each under-five child to have experience in a range of expressive arts and physical activities.

TARGETS OF OUTCOME

Through Birmingham City Education Department's Baseline Assessment for Nursery Schools/Units and Reception classes, to monitor the percentage of children at the respective development stages:

- with respect to language and literacy experience i.e:
  - speaking and listening
  - reading
  - writing

- with respect to mathematical experience:
  - algebra
  - number
  - shape and space
  - handling data

Appendix 3

THE PRIMARY GUARANTEE (OUTLINE)

TARGETS OF INPUT

- A % increase in the budget for primary school.
- A guarantee of consistent level of services for schools.
- Access to international and local networks and expertise at key moments in school improvement.

TARGETS OF PROCESS OR EXPERIENCE

- Every primary child will have a residential experience.
- Every six-year-old and nine-year-old takes part in a 'public performance'.
- All ten-year-olds carry out an environmental project.
- All parents of six- and eight-year-olds will be told what their child is particularly good at in the expressive arts and be encouraged to provide support.
- Each class of ten-year-olds in groups of 5 or 6 will write a story, illustrate it, turn it into a book and present it to five-year-olds.

TARGETS OF OUTCOME

Each school will audit at age seven and eleven the percentage of:

- apprentice readers
- foundation readers
- advanced readers
- independent readers

and agree targets for decreases in apprentice readers and increases in independent readers over the coming years.

Each school will audit at age seven and eleven the percentage of:

- apprentice mathematicians
- foundation mathematicians
- advanced mathematicians
- independent mathematicians

and agree targets for decreases in apprentice mathematicians and increases in independent mathematicians.

Appendix 4

THE SECONDARY GUARANTEE
(OUTLINE)

TARGETS OF INPUT

- A % increase in the budget for secondary schools in real terms.
- A guarantee of consistent support services to schools.
- Access to international, national and local networks and expertise at key moments in school improvement.

TARGETS OF PROCESS OR EXPERIENCE

- By the age of 12 each pupil should have had the opportunity to take part in a literacy performance
- By the age of 13 each pupil should have been involved in an activity which utilises IT skills and is demonstrable to parents.
- By the age of 14 each pupil should have had the opportunity to be involved in an artistic performance or physical activity involving the community.
- By the age of 14 each pupil should have been encouraged to self monitor their health and fitness profile.
- By the age of 15 each pupil should have had the opportunity to celebrate languages by using their knowledge of a European or community language, to support the activities of others.
- By the age of 16 every pupil should have had the opportunity for an out of school challenge involving self-organisation.
- By the age of 16 every pupil should have participated in a quality work experience placement as part of a planned programme of work-related activities.
- Throughout their total 11–16 school life pupils should have been encouraged to celebrate the City's wide range of cultures and religions, and have been taught to promote racial and sexual harmony, tolerance and justice.

- Post-16 students should follow courses which reflect their academic and vocational experiences and previous achievements, and have a good chance of achieving their objectives.

Pupils with special needs should have equal access to these experiences although the timing and detailed nature of them may vary according to individual need.

TARGETS OF OUTCOME

- At the age of 12 every pupil will have their level of attainment in mathematics and reading audited by the school, and be offered whatever support is necessary to develop those skills further.
- Each school will have self-generated targets of improved performance in the core subjects at the end of Key Stage 3.
- Each school will set targets to improve their examinations results against previous best performance.
- By the age of 16 every pupil should have produced an accredited Record of Achievement which incorporates a career plan and an IT-driven project.
- A successful transition will be attempted for each pupil to the next stage of continuing education or training/employment.

SELECTED READING

Ayers, W. (1993) *To Teach, the Journey of a Teacher*, Teachers' College Press, New York

Barber M (1996) *The Learning Game: Arguments for an Education Revolution*, Victor Gollancz, London

Barber M, Brighouse T (1992) *Partners in Change: Enhancing the Teaching Profession.* IPPR, London

Barth R (1990) *Improving Schools from Within*, Jossey-Bass, San Francisco

Brighouse T (1991) *What Makes a Good School?* Network Educational Press, Stafford

Brighouse T (1998) *Stories from the Inner City*. Questions Publishing, Birmingham

DfEE (1997) *Excellence in Schools*, DfEE, London

DfEE (1997) *School Performance and Extra Curricular Provision*, DfEE, London

DfEE (1998) *Extending Opportunity: A National Framework for Study Support*, DfEE, London

DfEE (1998) *From Targets to Action*, DfEE, London

DfEE/OFSTED (1996) *Setting Targets to Raise Standards: A Survey of Good Practice*, DfEE, London

Fink D, Stoll L (1996) *Changing our Schools*, Open University Press, Milton Keynes

Fried, R L (1995) *The Passionate Teacher*, Beacon Press, Boston

Fullan M G (1982) *The Meaning of Educational Change*, Teachers' College Press, New York

Fullan M G (1991) *The New Meaning of Educational Change*, Cassell, London

Fullan M G (1992) *Successful School Improvement*, Open University Press, Milton Keynes

Fullan M G (1992) *What's Worth Fighting for in Headship*, Open University Press, Milton Keynes

Gann N (1998) *Improving School Governance*, Falmer Press, London

Gardner H (1993) *Multiple Intelligences: The Theory in Practice*, Basic Books, New York

Gardner H (1993) *The Unschooled Mind*, Fontana Press, London

Goleman D (1996) *Emotional Intelligence: Why It matters More Than IQ*, Bloomsbury, London

Handy C R (1990) *Inside Organisations*, BBC Books, London

Handy C R (1994) *The Empty Raincoat: Making Sense of the Future*, Hutchinson, London

Hargreaves A (1994) *Changing Teachers, Changing Times*, Cassell, London

Hargreaves D, Hopkins D (1991) *The Empowered School*, Cassell, London

Hayden C (1997) *Children Excluded from Primary School*, Open University Press, Milton Keynes

Hopkins D, Ainscow M, West R (1994) *School Improvement in an Era of Change*, Cassell, London

Little J (1981) *The Power of Organisational Setting*, National Institute of Education, Washington DC

Louis K S, Miles M P (1990) *Improving the Urban High School*, Teachers' College Press, New York

MacGilchrist B, Myers K, Reed J (1997) *The Intelligent School*, Paul Chapman Publishing, London

Maden M, Hillman J (1996) *Success against the Odds*, Paul Hamlyn Foundation, National Education Commission, Routledge, London

Mortimore P, Sammons P, Stoll L, Lewis D, Ecob R (1988) *School Matters: The Junior Years*, Open Books, Wells

Rosenholtz S (1989) *Teachers' Workplace: The Social Organisation of Schools*, Langman, New York

Rubin L (1985) *Artistry in Teaching*, Random House, New York

Rutter M, Maugham B, Mortimore P, Ouston J (1979) *Fifteen Thousand Hours: Secondary Schools and their Effects on Pupils*, Open Books, London

Smith D, Tomlinson S (1989) *The School Effect*, Policy Institute, London

Tizard B (1988) *Young Children at School in the Inner City*, Laurence Erdbaum, London

West S (1993) *Educational Values for School Leadership*, Kogan Page, London

Woods D C, Orlik S (1994) *School Review and Inspection*, Kogan Page, London

Woods D C (ed.) (1997) *School Improvement Butterflies*, Questions Publishing, Birmingham

INDEX